CRAFT CHALLENGE

Dozens of Ways to Repurpose

Scarves

Nathalie Mornu

LARK CRAFTS

An Imprint of Sterling Publishing Co., Inc.
New York

WWW.LARKCRAFTS.COM

Technical Editor
Nancy Wood

Art Director
Megan Kirby

Art Assistant
Meagan Shirlen

Illustrators
Bernadette Wolf instructional

Orrin Lundgren templates

Photographer
Lynne Harty

Cover Designer
Megan Kirby

Editorial Assistant
Thom O'Hearn

Mornu, Nathalie.
  Craft challenge : dozens of ways to repurpose scarves / Nathalie Mornu. -- 1st ed.
    p. cm.
Includes index.
ISBN 978-1-60059-777-0 (pb-trade pbk. : alk. paper)
1. Scarves. 2. Textile crafts. 3. Sewing. I. Title.
TT699.M675 2011
646.4'8--dc22
                                        2010032949

10 9 8 7 6 5 4 3 2 1

First Edition

Published by Lark Crafts, An Imprint of
Sterling Publishing Co., Inc.
387 Park Avenue South, New York, NY 10016

Distributed in Canada by Sterling Publishing,
c/o Canadian Manda Group, 165 Dufferin Street
Toronto, Ontario, Canada M6K 3H6

Distributed in the United Kingdom by GMC Distribution Services,
Castle Place, 166 High Street, Lewes, East Sussex, England BN7 1XU

Distributed in Australia by Capricorn Link (Australia) Pty Ltd.,
P.O. Box 704, Windsor, NSW 2756 Australia

If you have questions or comments about this book, please contact:
Lark Crafts
67 Broadway
Asheville, NC 28801
828-253-0467

Manufactured in China

ISBN 13: 978-1-60059-777-0

For information about custom editions, special sales, premium, and corporate purchases, please contact the Sterling Special Sales Department at 800-805-5489 or specialsales@sterlingpub.com.

For information about desk and examination copies available to college and university professors, submit requests to academic@larkbooks.com. Our complete policy can be found at www.larkcrafts.com.

   **CRAFT CHALLENGE**

Dozens of Ways to Repurpose

Scarves

BONUS PROJECT

Toss Up

available **free** at
larkcrafts.com/bonus

contents

BONUS PROJECT
Picture Perfect
available **free** at
larkcrafts.com/bonus

introduction

Don't you love showing off your cleverness and whimsy by taking something old and refashioning it into something way cool and fresh? Well, the craft-blogging community feels that way, too; these crafters are simply mad for online challenges that transform great old fabrics into something else altogether wonderful. And as if *that* wasn't enough fun, they then post photos of this made-over cuteness online for everyone to admire! Now you can join them and our team of project designers, who've discovered scarves as the perfect bit of cloth for making a craft project.

Scarves come in a wide range of fabric types, and in terrific retro graphics chock full of repurposing potential. Just flip through these pages: Is that a heavy wool muffler on page 77, or the cutest plush bunny ever? Does page 57 feature mod scarves, or totally cool skirts? And on page 62—wispy headscarf, or light-as-air earrings?

The 30 projects in this book breathe all kinds of new life into a common accessory. If you're looking to add some pizzazz to your home, make a scarf-draped lampshade that lends a touch of boho chic to a room, or turn a handful of ho-hum scarves into breezy curtains. If your wardrobe needs jazzing up, choose from accessories including an oversized coin purse, a pretty knotted necklace, or a wide belt. And clothes! Whip up a summery hippie-girl dress or some flirty short shorts; embellish a tank top with fluttery strips of scarf material; and stitch an exotic-looking skirt in no time flat. Thirty projects not enough for you? You'll find two more bonus projects at www. larkcrafts.com.

If you're the type of person who fingers gossamer scarves in vintage stores, wishing you could buy them all, or who pores over the designer scarves in department store cases just to admire the gorgeous prints and luxurious silks, this book is for you. Come join the fun! Start with the best part: the hunt for the perfect scarf. Then follow along with the step-by-step instructions to upcycle it to your heart's delight. (The Basics section will serve as a refresher course if your sewing skills feel rusty, and some of the projects require no sewing at all—just cutting, gluing, and knotting.) Finally, flaunt pictures of the results to your appreciative friends online.

Enough talk. Get a little inspiration from this book, gather up a scarf or two or ten, and prove your brilliance with scissors, glue, and thread.

scarf basics

the goods

The greatest fun of repurposing fabric is the search for that perfect diamond-in-the-rough just waiting to be transformed into something else altogether wonderful—and the variety of scarves out there for you to discover is absolutely mind blowing! You'll find head scarves of all different weights and colors, warm woolen neck scarves, and lighter-than-air silk scarves. Vintage scarves are a great source for retro graphics, and you might even come across designer scarves and souvenir scarves sold long ago to a tourist visiting foreign lands. Polyester scarves combine well with other fabrics to make great projects. Translucent jewel colors and bold floral patterns with geometric borders are all part of the palette available to play with. And long, flowing scarves from India, with metallic surfaces, sequins, and beads, are enough to transport you to another part of the globe.

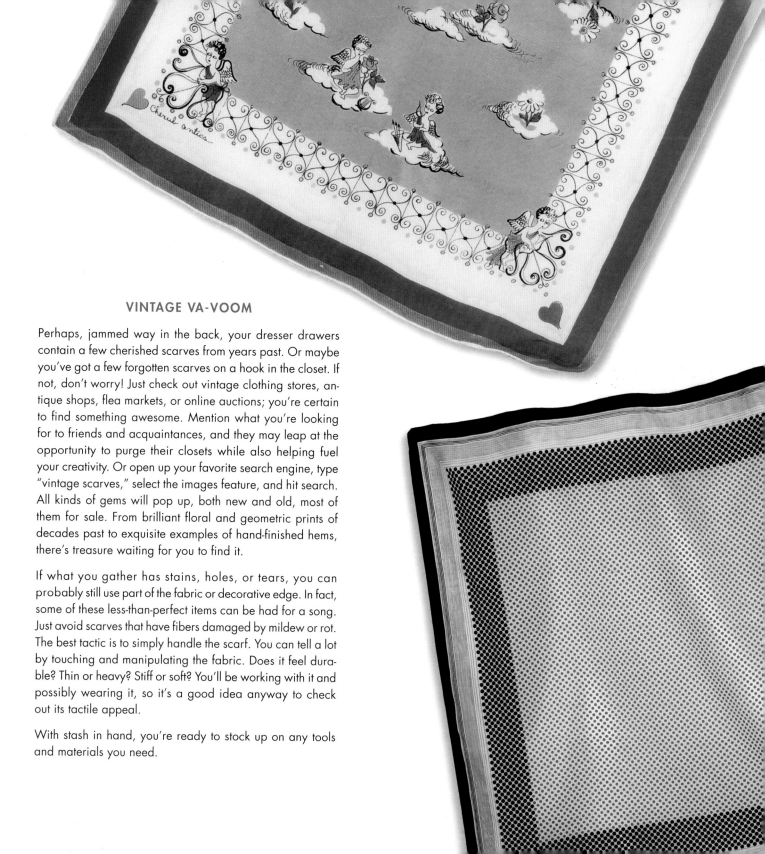

VINTAGE VA-VOOM

Perhaps, jammed way in the back, your dresser drawers contain a few cherished scarves from years past. Or maybe you've got a few forgotten scarves on a hook in the closet. If not, don't worry! Just check out vintage clothing stores, antique shops, flea markets, or online auctions; you're certain to find something awesome. Mention what you're looking for to friends and acquaintances, and they may leap at the opportunity to purge their closets while also helping fuel your creativity. Or open up your favorite search engine, type "vintage scarves," select the images feature, and hit search. All kinds of gems will pop up, both new and old, most of them for sale. From brilliant floral and geometric prints of decades past to exquisite examples of hand-finished hems, there's treasure waiting for you to find it.

If what you gather has stains, holes, or tears, you can probably still use part of the fabric or decorative edge. In fact, some of these less-than-perfect items can be had for a song. Just avoid scarves that have fibers damaged by mildew or rot. The best tactic is to simply handle the scarf. You can tell a lot by touching and manipulating the fabric. Does it feel durable? Thin or heavy? Stiff or soft? You'll be working with it and possibly wearing it, so it's a good idea anyway to check out its tactile appeal.

With stash in hand, you're ready to stock up on any tools and materials you need.

So Very Vera

Anyone hunting for vintage scarves is bound to come across the Vera brand: her textiles are everywhere, their graphics are immediately recognizable, the prints and colors are beautiful...and there's the unmistakable identifying signature.

Textile designer Vera Neumann and her husband, George, started a business a few years after World War II ended making silkscreened placemats in their New York City kitchen. The war created shortages of cotton and linen, but the surplus of parachute silk gave Vera the idea of applying her designs—dots, geometric designs, painted flourishes, and florals, all of them bold, colorful, and graphic—to scarves. Within a short time, Printex, as the successful company was called, outgrew first their apartment and then a Midtown Manhattan loft, so they moved to a run-down mansion in Ossining, New York. The couple lived in four rooms and devoted the rest of the manor to the printing plant. All aspects of manufacture, from design to printing and finishing, took place there.

By the '50s, with business booming, Vera had assembled a team of designers who translated the original drawings she made on 36-inch (91.4 cm) scarves into other merchandise. The team developed five- to six hundred designs each year. In the '60s, in addition to scarves and household linens, they began designing a line of clothing based on that same yard-long (91.4 cm) format but engineered from the get-go with a finished garment in mind.

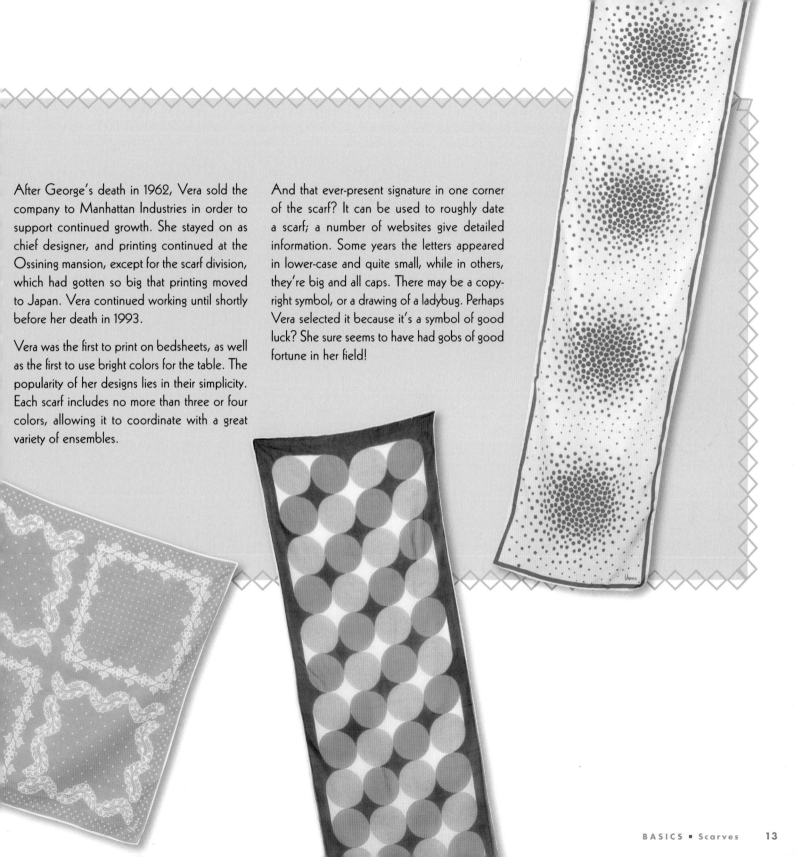

After George's death in 1962, Vera sold the company to Manhattan Industries in order to support continued growth. She stayed on as chief designer, and printing continued at the Ossining mansion, except for the scarf division, which had gotten so big that printing moved to Japan. Vera continued working until shortly before her death in 1993.

Vera was the first to print on bedsheets, as well as the first to use bright colors for the table. The popularity of her designs lies in their simplicity. Each scarf includes no more than three or four colors, allowing it to coordinate with a great variety of ensembles.

And that ever-present signature in one corner of the scarf? It can be used to roughly date a scarf; a number of websites give detailed information. Some years the letters appeared in lower-case and quite small, while in others, they're big and all caps. There may be a copyright symbol, or a drawing of a ladybug. Perhaps Vera selected it because it's a symbol of good luck? She sure seems to have had gobs of good fortune in her field!

Basic Sewing Kit

All of the projects in this book call for the Sewing Kit outlined below, so gather these items before you start.

- Sewing machine and needles
- Hand-sewing needles
- Thread
- Straight pins and safety pins
- Sewing scissors or shears
- Rotary cutter, mat, and ruler
- Craft scissors (for cutting paper)
- Paper for drawing and adapting templates (tissue, gift wrap, or kraft paper are all fine)
- Stabilizer
- Tape measure
- Seam ripper
- Iron and ironing board
- Pressing cloth
- Pencil with an eraser
- Fabric marker
- Point turner (such as a chopstick)

the notions

It's pretty easy to get carried away with materials and tools. (Warning: people who've caught the sewing bug sometimes force their families to eat standing up in the kitchen because they've appropriated the dining room table!) But here's the thing: You won't need much to make any of the projects in this book. If you're new to sewing, read on for practical advice about what to collect to get started.

SEWING MACHINE

Forget fancy machines. Look for one that just has the basic, utilitarian stitches: straight, satin, and zigzag. Fact is, you could hand sew every project in this book if you weren't in such a rush to finish your cute, *cute*, **cute** project! (Besides, for the strongest seams and fastest results, there's nothing like a sewing machine.)

sewing machine

THREAD

Match thread to the fabric content. In other words, use quality cotton or cotton-wrapped thread with cotton fabric and nylon or polyester thread with synthetic fabric.

Anytime you glance at a bargain bin of thread and start feeling tempted to buy some, just remind yourself that you get exactly what you pay for, and walk away quickly. Cheap thread is weak and it has barely visible slubs that prevent it from sliding easily through fabric and a machine needle's eye.

thread

CUTTING TOOLS

Sewing's a lot more fun when you expand your collection beyond just a pair of sharp scissors. Those are a great starting point, of course, and you really need little more, but specialty cutting tools offer speed and precision you just can't get any other way.

SCISSORS

Two types are essential in every sewing kit: plain old craft scissors (the kind you probably already have tucked away in a drawer) and a sharp pair of shears with 8- to 10-inch (20.3 to 25.4 cm) blades and fine tips. You can find the latter at any sewing supply store. It's worth it to invest in quality: a good pair lasts a lifetime. Look for a pair with a screw at the base of the blades that can be tightened as time goes by, for a better cut. Never, *ever* use this fine pair for cutting paper! The wood fibers of paper will dull the blades in no time flat and render them useless on fabric. (Don't fret if someone—ahem—messes up, cuts paper with your shears, and dulls the blades; you can have them sharpened.)

SEAM RIPPER

Check the tool kit that came with your sewing machine: most machines are sold with one of these. A seam ripper is indispensable for "reverse sewing," as some stitchers call the act of ripping out stitching bloopers.

seam ripper

ROTARY CUTTER, QUILTING RULER, AND MAT

A rotary cutter makes straight, long cuts as easy as pie. The thick edge of a clear quilter's ruler can serve as an excellent guide for rolling the cutter along the fabric, but it's not essential to use this tool. You must, however, always place a self-healing mat underneath the fabric before you start cutting: the rotary blade is sharp enough to destroy an unprotected surface but fragile enough to be easily damaged. When you find yourself pressing down on the cutter—or notice it skipping spots—it's time to replace the blade. This trio—blade, mat, and ruler—forms a great team for squaring up fabrics. Some of the vintage scarves you find may be stretched out of shape, so line them up on the mat grid and trim away any wavy edges.

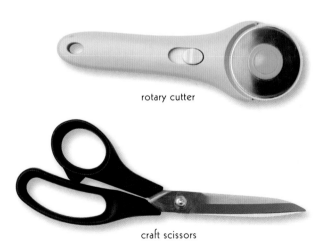

rotary cutter

craft scissors

NEEDLES

Overwhelmed by all the choices? Just start with the most basic machine, hand, and embroidery needles.

MACHINE NEEDLES

You can get away with a universal 80/12 sewing machine needle for most of your stitching. For delicate fabrics, like really fine scarves, switch to a finer needle—about a 60/8—and make sure that it's a type called a sharp. Start every sewing project with a new needle. They're cheap, so get a whole bunch and switch to a new one often. You probably won't notice that your needle is ready for the trash until a dull point or a burr on a shaft snags a thread in your scarf...and then you're stuck fixing the damage.

machine needles

HAND-SEWING AND EMBROIDERY NEEDLES

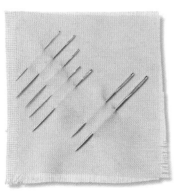

The projects in this book aren't rocket science. Don't worry about the type of needle to use, or the numbering system labeling needle sizes; just buy a package containing an assortment, and start experimenting. You'll quickly gravitate to a favorite length, size, and type.

hand-sewing and embroidery needles

ETCETERA

No matter the task—from marking fabric to making a seam—there's a tool or material that'll make the job easier. Here's a rundown of the notions that are essential or most helpful. Stitchers tend to accumulate these at an amazing rate–and misplace them just as fast. (I do, at any rate!) To keep a handle on it all, store everything in one place, preferably in something portable.

STRAIGHT PINS

All-purpose dressmaker's pins are your best bet. To work with especially delicate fabric you might want to indulge in a box of silk pins, which are finer. Wanna start an argument? Ask a couple of stitchers the correct way to insert pins through fabric layers! Some place pins along—or parallel to—seam lines, whereas others prefer a perpendicular placement.

straight pins

tip

While sewing with a machine, always remove pins as your fabric enters the stitching area. Hitting a pin can throw off the machine's timing and snap or dull the needle.

fabric markers

FABRIC MARKERS

These are just the thing for making lines or marks on fabric—whether for cutting, sewing, or making decorative designs to stitch over. There are two different kinds available. In one type, the inks fade on their own—within 24 hours or so according to the manufacturers, although it's often sooner. (With this type of marker, don't wait too long to complete the project or the guidelines will disappear.) With the other type of marker, the ink lasts longer, and washes out by soaking the fabric in cool water. Note: Disappearing inks can be quirky. Test your marker on a scrap of fabric to make sure that the ink does completely disappear. Also, remove the marks (either with water or by air-drying) before applying interfacing or a stabilizer to the fabric—the chemicals in some products can make the marks permanent when pressed with a hot iron!

Map Scarves

While map scarves certainly fit in the category of souvenirs (page 19), they're so delightful that they need singling out here.

Among the gems you might spot while you're sleuthing in scarf-land:

- The romanticized plan of the Métro and main attractions of the City of Light (at right). *Très joli, non?*

- A very functional map of the New York City subway system.

- A scarf undoubtedly related to Alaska's joining the union in 1959 (at bottom right). This bad boy is a trove of information. At the center, a map of the state depicts geographical features, major cities, and graphics representing industry (such as mining and fishing) and wildlife. The state flag and the state bird—the willow ptarmigan—are featured, and the border includes the state flower, the forget-me-not. The best part, though, has got to be the images in the corners. Just look at the cheeks on those kids!

- Charts of invented places, such as a scarf featuring the trio of Couture Islands called Cake, Chocolate, and Juicy, located in the Heiress Ocean; another scarf diagramming the site of pirate treasure; and one scarf map that seems to be a mashup of quadrants from unrelated and little-known parts of the world—if they exist at all!

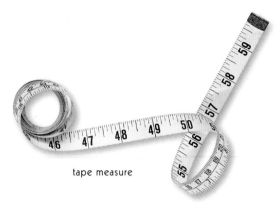

tape measure

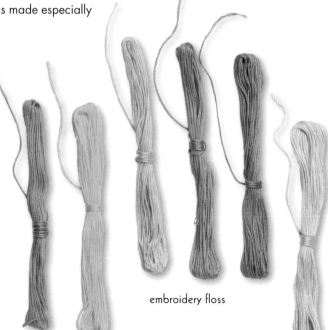

mini iron

TAPE MEASURE

For accurate measuring along curves, stand the tape measure on one of its edges.

IRON AND IRONING BOARD

Use what you have. If you want to get fancy, invest in a quality iron; it's heavier so you get a better press faster. Craft and fabric shops sell mini irons that get into tight spaces like corners.

PRESSING CLOTH

When pressing delicate scarves, you don't want to burn or damage the fabric. The solution? Lay a pressing cloth, either dry or damp, over the scarf before applying the iron. You can use a piece of clean cotton fabric or buy special cloths made especially for this purpose.

DRESSMAKER'S HAM

Speaking of pressing, a dressmaker's ham is not an essential item, but you may find it handy for pressing curvy items, such as the Shorty tap pants on page 30. Traditionally used for pressing darts and curved seams, this firmly packed item is shaped somewhat like a football, and available in sewing stores and online.

EMBROIDERY FLOSS

Floss consists of six loosely twisted strands made from cotton, silk, or other fibers. Cut a length of floss no longer than 20 inches (50.8 cm), and then pull the desired number of strands from one end.

needle threader

needle threader

Can't get those renegade threads through your needle? Use this little tool. Put the wire loop through the needle, insert the thread into the loop, pull back, and *voilà*!

embroidery floss

Souvenir Scarves

What kind of tchotchke should you bring Aunt Mabel back from your vacation? Well, le'ssee, you could get her a T-shirt, or a mug, a key ring perhaps, or even a tea towel…but wouldn't a scarf be nicer?

Countries, cities, states, and even islands are all represented on souvenir scarves: They'll feature images of the sights of San Francisco, Rome, or Paris, for example, or the landmarks in London. A wonderful vintage scarf from New Zealand is cram-jammed with information, showing an outline of the islands, drawings of a kiwi bird and three types of native flowers, tikis, and portraits of two tattooed Maori chiefs in traditional dress. An old souvenir scarf from Brazil shows a garish green sketch of a dancer wearing a fruit hat.

There's an abundant supply of Niagara Falls scarves available from online auctions. Hunt carefully, though, and you'll find some real unusual stuff, such as the acetate scarf sold at Sam Snyder's Water Follies in 1955, featuring a bevy of be-capped bathing beauties in pale blue suits surrounded by drawings of buff guys diving, clowns carrying surf boards, and splashing water. You can find scarves from other amusement parks, too, including one printed with a drawing of the Ferris wheel in Vienna, and another from Busch Gardens. Prefer wildlife to roller coasters? Then you might like a scarf from the Serengeti National Park better, or one from Yellowstone.

STABILIZER

There are all kinds of commercial stabilizers available, in a number of different weights and designed for different purposes. For the projects in this book, you'll simply pin slippery scarf fabrics to stabilizer to keep the material under control while you cut or sew with it. When using stabilizer during stitching, you want a type that you can either tear off or dissolve after sewing.

While you can purchase both tear-away and soluble stabilizers, I see no reason to waste good money. I use tissue paper. I always have patterns I have no intention of making, and that works great to stabilize tricky fabrics. (For all you thrifty types who save gift-wrap, tissue paper can be ironed on low heat to take out the wrinkles.)

INTERFACING

Areas of fabric that need a bit of strength can be reinforced on the underside with interfacing. This flat, plain material is sold in many weights, or degrees of firmness. Choose a weight that's suitable for the type of fabric you're using. You also pick the interfacing by application: sew-in or fusible. The easiest type to use is fusible because it's attached to the entire back of the fabric with a gluelike resin that's activated by pressing with an iron. Sew-in interfacing, on the other hand, is secured by catching the edges in seams.

three weights of interfacing

BATTING AND STUFFING

This puffy stuff is sold as batting (which comes flattened out, in lengths) or stuffing (which comes stuffed in a bag). Cotton tends to be flat and yields a folksy, homespun effect; high-loft polyester is puffier and more resilient. There's even a type of batting that's fusible on one side so you can bond it to fabric. Unless a project calls for a specific type, go with whatever you fancy, or whatever your local store sells.

tip

Some fusible interfacing is designed for a temporary bond. In other words, the resin releases from the back of the fabric after the project has been washed a few times. Make sure you *don't* buy this type for the projects in this book.

BIAS BINDING

Bias binding is used mainly to finish raw fabric edges by enclosing them. To make it, a woven fabric is cut into strips, then folded and pressed. Since the strips are cut on the pliant bias grain of the fabric, bias tape, as it's also called, is stretchy so it lies smoothly on curved edges as well as on straight ones. The double-fold bias binding called for in this book can be purchased in various solid colors, prints, and metallics, or you can make your own from just about any smooth, lightweight fabric. To make your own, see page 25.

bias tape

GROMMETS

Grommets, like the ones in the Kashmir window panels on page 105, or the eyelets in Hang It Up on page 102, may look intimidating, but they're really a breeze to install. Look for kits that contain setting tools, usually a special pair of pliers or a mallet, and just follow the brief, simple instructions on the packet.

grommet setting tools

grommets

the nitty-gritty

With your supplies rounded up, it's time to transform that scarf into something really cool. This part of the book gives you information on the techniques you'll need. Before starting any project, read through all the instructions, start to finish; that can help avoid mistakes. Anytime you're unsure of a technique, refer back to this section.

USING A TEMPLATE

Some of the projects call for a template or pattern, a shape that needs to be cut from the fabric. Just turn to the page number given and make photocopies of the ones you need for your chosen project, enlarging them if that's called for. Cut these paper templates out with your craft scissors and then switch to shears to cut as many fabric shapes as you need.

MARKING AND TRANSFERRING ONTO FABRIC

Some of the patterns and all of the embroidery designs have lines or marks that need to be made on the fabric shapes. There are plenty of ways to do this, including using a light box, chalk, or transfer paper. The number one problem that stitchers encounter is ending up with a reverse image on the fabric. In other words, the lines and marks are on the left when they should be on the right, and vice versa. When in doubt, make a quick paper mock-up of the process you're using to ensure you're orienting everything the right way.

HAND-SEWING STITCHES

You might have to do a bit of hand sewing to complete the project you like, but it won't be a lot—honest. (On the other hand, if you find hand sewing relaxing, go ahead and make all of your seams this way!) Start by threading your needle and then secure the end with a knot or three tiny stitches in the same place in the fabric. At the end of the sewing, make another three tiny stitches before you cut off the excess thread.

Basting Stitch Make very long, straight stitches to temporarily hold together fabric layers. Because basting stitches are long, they're easy to pull out after they've served their purpose.

Running Stitch Create this stitch by weaving the needle through the fabric at evenly spaced intervals (figure 1).

Whipstitch Used for binding edges to prevent raveling, a whipstitch sews edges together very tightly. Working from the wrong side, insert the needle perpendicular to the fabric edge, over and over again. The stitches will look slanted (figure 2).

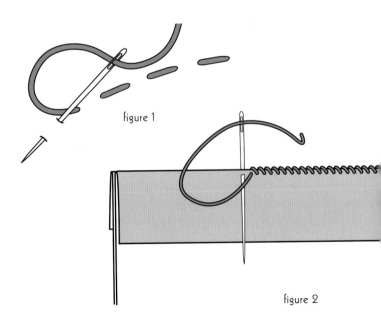

figure 1

figure 2

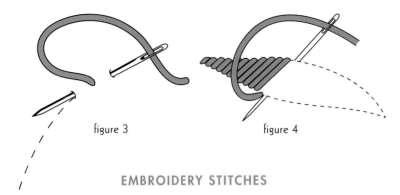

figure 3   figure 4

EMBROIDERY STITCHES

Start with a length of floss or very narrow silk ribbon—and don't knot the end. The best way to secure embroidery is to leave the last 1 or 2 inches (2.5 or 5.1 cm) on the underside and then lay this short end across the back so it gets caught in the subsequent stitching.

Backstitch A sturdier version of the straight stitch, the backstitch is good for stuffed projects, holding the seam under pressure (figure 3). Backstitches are also used to embroider decorative lines.

Satin Stitch The satin stitch is composed of parallel rows of straight stitches; it's often used to fill in an outline (figure 4).

MACHINE STITCHES

Machine stitching is the easiest, fastest way to permanently join fabric shapes. (Okay, well, really, gluing might be faster and easier, but it looks awful!) Follow these basic steps:

1 *Backstitch* at the start of the seam line by sewing forward for ¼ inch (6 mm), in reverse back to the beginning, and then forward again.

2 Machine stitch along the seam line using the recommended *seam allowance* width (the seam allowance is the fabric between the seam line and the raw edge), removing pins as they get close to the needle. The instructions in this book give you the suitable seam allowance width for each project. Let the machine do the work of pulling the fabric along.

3 To stitch around a corner, keep the needle down at the corner point and pivot the fabric. Backstitch at the end of the seam line so that the stitching doesn't unravel.

Straight Stitch This stitch is used more than any other. Unless the project instructions give you a different setting, use a medium-length straight stitch—about 2.5 mm long or 12 spi (stitches per inch). Whatever system your machine has, you'll be in good shape if you dial into something in the middle of the offered range. Set the stitch width to 0.

Topstitch No mystery here: topstitching is just straight stitching worked with the right side up, usually through several fabric thicknesses and positioned near an edge or a seam line so it's decorative.

Edgestitch This is exactly like topstitching with a minor twist. When you edgestitch, you sew as close to the fabric edge as you can. It is less decorative and more functional than topstitching—it's one stitch that's happy to work invisibly on the sidelines.

Zigzag Stitch If you don't own pinking shears, you can use medium-length, wide-width zigzag stitching to prevent fraying along fabric edges. Or simply use this as a decorative topstitch.

Satin Stitch This stitch can be done by machine as well as by hand (see Embroidery Stitches at left). It's often accomplished by using one of the buttonhole stitch settings. Check your sewing machine manual for instructions.

MAKING BUTTONHOLES

Machine stitching around a buttonhole prevents the cut fabric edges from stretching and fraying. Most sewing machines make a buttonhole with little more than a twist of a dial and a presser foot change. You won't need to make buttonholes for any of these projects, but if your machine gives you the option, you might want to use a buttonhole setting or satin stitch when making the Waisting Time belt on page 65.

CLIPPING CORNERS AND CURVES

A well-made seam is flat and smooth when it's right side out. (The exceptions, of course, are intentionally gathered fabric and other special effects, but we're not dealing with that here.) Seam allowances can mess with this perfection because excess fabric has either bunched up or stretched out on the underside, particularly at corners and curves. The solutions to these problems are simple.

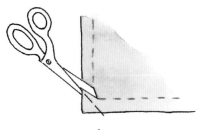

figure 5

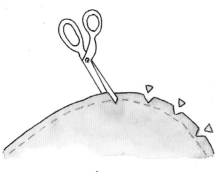

figure 6

figure 7

Corners Snip diagonally across the tip of a corner to remove excess seam allowance (figure 5). To avoid weakening the seam, stay at least ⅛ inch (3 mm) away from the stitching.

Curves For fabric on an outside curve, notch the seam allowance in several places (figure 6). Use the tips of your sharpest scissors to snip through the seam allowances perpendicular to the seam line. Make sure that you snip to—but not through—the stitching. Space the snips ½ inch (1.3 cm) apart along the curved portion of the seam line. If necessary, make more snips until the seam line appears smooth.

For fabric on an *inside curve*, just make clips into the seam allowance (figure 7). This will allow the seam allowance to spread out a bit when you turn the fabric right side out, giving a smoother curve.

MAKING A HEM

For finishing a raw edge, the most straightforward solution is a double-fold hem. The hem can be as wide or as narrow as you wish. Fold the edge ¼ inch (6 mm) to the inside and press it. The second fold can be anything from ¼ to 1 inch (6 mm to 2.5 cm) or more. Press again, then stitch in place. If you're in a hurry and the fabric is cooperating, you don't need to press it each time. But at the very least, pin the fold in place and check that it's even all the way around before you stitch. When stitching a scarf with a finished edge, often you only need a single-fold hem. The instructions are the same, just fold once instead of twice.

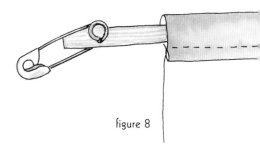

figure 8

MAKING A CASING

Some of the projects call for either elastic or a drawstring, and that means making a casing. The process is pretty much the same as for a double-fold hem. Start by folding under the edge of the fabric ¼ inch (6 mm) or less. The next fold is determined by the width of the elastic or tie you plan to use. If you're using ½-inch (1.3 cm) elastic, make the next fold that width plus about ⅛ inch (3 mm). This will give you some wiggle room to insert the elastic (usually with the help of a safety pin attached to one end), and will give the elastic some breathing room (figure 8). Don't add too much extra, though, or the elastic will likely twist in the casing. Even non-roll elastic has its limits.

If you're using a drawstring instead of elastic, while making the casing you can double or triple the width of the second fold. Twisting isn't an issue with a drawstring, and the gathers look nicer if the casing isn't too narrow or tight.

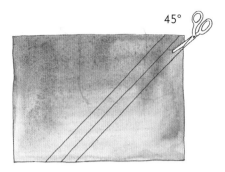

figure 9

figure 10

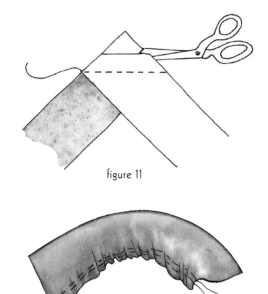

figure 11

figure 12

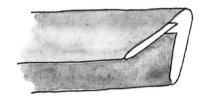

figure 13

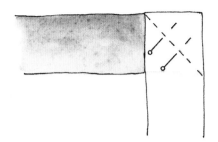

figure 14

MAKING BIAS TAPE

You can enclose the raw edges of one or more fabric layers with bias tape to create a clean, sturdy edge that's also decorative. Store-bought bias tape is handy, but for a perfect color match, here's how to make your own double-fold binding. Steps 3 and 4 are also good steps to follow for making a strap.

1 Decide how wide you want the finished binding to be. Multiply that by four, and cut several strips that width on the bias (figure 9). For example, to make finished bias tape ¼ inch (6 mm) wide, cut bias strips 1 inch (2.5 cm) wide.

2 Stitch the strips end to end until you have one strip long enough to cover the raw edge you have in mind. For a professional look, and to reduce bulk, stitch the strips together on the diagonal (figure 10). To cut down on bulk later, snip off the corners, parallel to the seam allowance (figure 11). Open up the seams and press.

3 Fold and press the entire length of the strip right down the middle. Open up the strip and fold each of the sides in toward the pressed center (figure 12). You now have single-fold bias tape. (If you want to make quick work of this step, invest in a bias tape maker.)

4 To make double-fold bias tape, fold along the center line and press again (figure 13). If making a strap, open the tape up again to turn under the short ends, refold, then stitch on all open sides.

MAKING RUFFLES

A strip to add as a ruffle should be at least two and a half times longer than the edge it will embellish. Sew two parallel rows of basting stitches along one long edge. Don't trim the thread ends; instead, carefully pull them to gather the fabric to the desired length (figure 14). On all four ends of the basting stitches, pull the bobbin thread to the front and knot it with the other thread, close to the fabric. Adjust the gathers evenly.

BINDING AN EDGE

Here's how to apply either prepackaged double-fold bias tape or bias strips that you've made yourself. But first, a couple of handy little tricks for attaching binding:

- Look closely at double-fold tape and you'll see that the folded edges aren't exactly the same width. The idea is to enclose the raw edge with the narrower fold on the top, or right, side of the fabric, with the wider fold in back. When you stitch along the top, you automatically catch the back. This makes things so much easier!

- Apply tiny dots of fabric glue here and there (use it sparingly) to hold the bias tape in place as you go, using pins only in the areas where you feel it's necessary, such as curves and corners. When the glue is dry, stitch along the front edge of the bias tape.

- In order to really make sure to catch the back edge in your stitching, use a zigzag instead of a straight stitch.

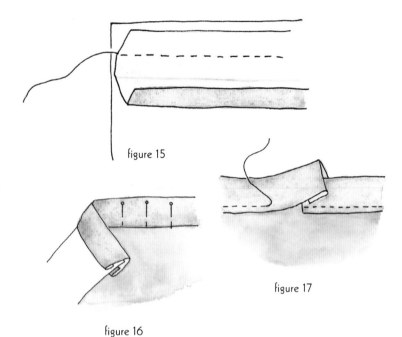

figure 15

figure 16

figure 17

To make it clearer what's going on, the first two illustrations show the binding beginning at the corner of the fabric. When lapping the ends, however, you should start somewhere along a side, not at a corner.

1 Begin by sewing a row of stay-stitching ¾ inch (1.9 cm) away from all the raw edges to bind. Trim back the seam allowance so that only ⅛ inch (3 mm) remains beyond the line of stay-stitching.

2 Measure the distance to bind, add 5 inches (12.7 cm), and cut this length of binding strip. Pin one raw edge of the binding to the raw edge of the fabric as shown, on the wrong side (figure 15). Stitch along the edge in the crease of the bias tape. Stop stitching 3 inches (7.6 cm) from the starting point and clip the loose end so that 1 inch (2.5 cm) of tape overlaps the part that's sewn down.

3 Turn the bias tape to the right side of the fabric, fold the raw edge of the tape under, and pin it down (figure 16). Machine stitch near the fold of the bias tape, stopping 2 inches (5.1 cm) from the starting point.

4 To tidy up the ends, lap them by folding the loose tail under ½ inch (1.3 cm) (figure 17). Finish stitching the binding.

MITERING A CORNER

There are many ways of turning a corner with bias tape. Here's a simple solution that works well, as seen on the Mosaic quilt on page 98. When using prepackaged bias tape, make sure the wider fold is in the back (page 25).

1 Enclose the raw edge on one side of the fabric and use a zigzag stitch to attach the binding to the top raw edge (figure 18). The zigzag stitch helps assure that you catch the edge of the binding in the back of the fabric.

2 Make a diagonal fold in the bias tape as you tuck it behind the top raw edge of the fabric (figure 19). Align the center fold of the bias tape with the raw edge of the fabric.

3 Fold the top of the bias tape over the top raw edge and continue stitching with a zigzag stitch (figure 20).

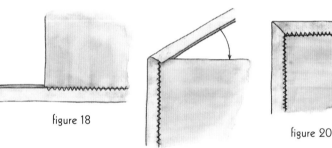

figure 18

figure 19

figure 20

FRENCH SEAMS

This seam completely encloses the raw fabric edges and looks as polished on the wrong side as it does on the right. You need a seam allowance of at least ⅝ inch (1.6 cm) to accomplish this seam.

1 Trust me, here, because this is going to seem incorrect at first. With the wrong sides of the fabric together, make the seam ⅜ inch (1 cm) from the raw edge. Trim away half of the seam allowance (figure 21).

2 Press the seam open, then fold it so the right sides face together (figure 22). Press to make a crease along the stitch line.

figure 21

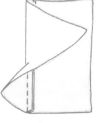

figure 22

Commemorative Scarves

As you look around for great old scarves to repurpose, you're sure to come across some unusual ones commemorating people and events. Scarves honoring Queen Elizabeth's coronation and particularly her Jubilee are pretty common, at least online. So are scarves celebrating World's Fairs.

Among some of the other offerings you may find:

- A sporty red scarf with white pictograms of humans engaged in the sports played at the 1976 Olympics.

- A red, white, and blue number marking the American Bicentennial.

- In keeping with the patriotic theme, the American presidents, including a scarf bedecked with nothing but their signatures.

- Scarves that memorialize Prince Charles and Lady Diana's 1981 wedding.

- Rock bands and musicians, such as Elvis or Kiss, and their concert tours.

- Sporting events, such as the Kentucky Derby, and teams, like the New York Giants.

- Various jamborees.

And of course, companies print scarves celebrating their product or service. As you look around, it won't take long to come across some truly weird scarves, like the headscarf printed with the Greyhound Bus Lines logo: an all-around border of turquoise greyhounds racing one behind the other. Another, dating from the '40s and printed in brown, orange, pale green, and white, is covered in sketches showing the key scenes from *Gone with the Wind*. Have you always dreamed of owning a scarf covered with the logos of various car rental agencies? Believe it or not, it exists!

Wear

Shorty

Tie One On

On the Edge

Garden Club

Stay Cool

Breezy

Hits the Spot

Bombay Dreams

Flutters

Double Trouble

Shorty

put the frill back
in your life.

◇◇◇◇◇◇◇◇◇◇◇◇◇◇◇◇◇◇

designed by Nathalie Mornu

What You Do

1

Mount a new needle in the sewing machine and make sure you have enough stabilizer (page 20) on hand to use when sewing up the project.

2

Enlarge the patterns on page 125 and cut them out.

3

Press the main fabric scarf, then fold it in half. Move the pattern around on the scarf, considering all the different places the prints could end up on the shorts. As you mull it over, be sure to stay on the grain. Pin the pattern pieces where you like, then cut them out (two of each piece). Mark each of the back pieces with a safety pin.

What You Need

For the main fabric, 1 scarf at least 36 inches (91.4 cm) square

For the ruffled trim, 1 sheer scarf at least 48 x 7 inches (121.9 x 17.8 cm)

1¼ yard (1.1 m) of elastic, ¼-inch wide (6 mm)

Dressmaker's ham (page 18)

Basic Sewing Kit (page 14)

Finished Sizes
Small, Medium, Large

Seam Allowance
½ inch (1.3 cm) unless otherwise noted

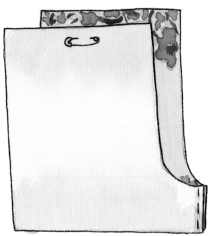

figure 1

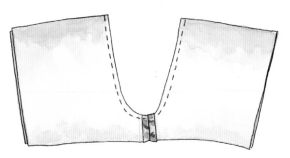

figure 2

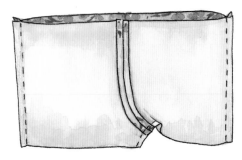

figure 3

4

With right sides facing, stitch one front piece to one back piece at the inner leg (figure 1). Stitch over the same line to reinforce the seam. Repeat with the remaining pair of pieces. Tear away the stabilizer. Press, then zigzag the raw edges.

5

Pin the front and back together, right sides facing, matching the seams. Stitch the crotch seam (figure 2). Stitch over the same line to reinforce the seam. Tear away the stabilizer, press, and zigzag the raw edges.

6

With right sides together, stitch the front and back together along one side. Do the same on the other side (figure 3). Reinforce the seams by stitching over them again, then tear off the stabilizer, press, and zigzag the raw edges. Set aside the layers.

7

To make the ruffles, cut the sheer scarf into two pieces that measure 48 x 3½ inches (121.9 x 8.9 cm). To sidestep the need to hem these strips, plan one long side along an outside finished edge. Gather the strip 1½ inches (3.8 cm) away from the *finished edge* of each scarf. Make another line of stitching ⅛ inch (3 mm) away from and parallel to the original line of stitches. Tear away the stabilizer and, on the side closer to the raw edge, trim to ¼ inch (6 mm) away from the pair of stitch lines.

8

Gather the ruffles until they're the same length as the circumference of one of the leg openings. Pin one ruffle to each leg opening, right sides together, matching raw edges and overlapping the ends of the ruffles at the crotch seams. With the machine set to a medium length, stitch the ruffles to the pants. Remove the stabilizer, zigzag all the raw edges, and press the seams away from the ruffles.

9

Topstitch the leg openings, ⅛ inch (3 mm) away from the seam where the ruffles connect to the bottom edge of the shorts. Set aside.

10

Cut a piece of elastic that fits snugly but comfortably around your waist. Fold over the top of the shorts to make a casing (page 24) and stitch it, leaving an opening for the elastic. Remove the stabilizer and run the elastic through the casing; as you work, don't allow it to twist. Stitch the ends of the elastic together with a ½-inch (1.3 cm) overlap. Stitch the casing shut.

Tie One On

fight the heat in a swingy, draping dress.

◇◇◇◇◇◇◇◇◇◇◇◇◇◇◇◇◇◇◇◇◇◇◇◇◇

designed by Jamie Powell

What You Need

3 scarves measuring 26 to 28 inches (66 to 71.1 cm) square, *all the same size*

2 yards (1.8 m) of ribbon, 1 inch (2.5 cm) wide

3 yards (2.7 m) of double-fold bias tape, ¼ inch (6 mm) wide

Basic Sewing Kit (page 14)

Finished Size
One size fits most, with adjustments to seams

Seam Allowance
¼ inch (6 mm) unless otherwise noted

What You Do

1

Mount a new needle in the sewing machine and make sure you have enough stabilizer (page 20) on hand for the project.

2

Decide which two scarves will be the front of your dress (scarves 1 and 2). Lay them out flat, on top of each other, right sides facing.

3

Decide which side of your scarf will become the center front seam. On this side, measure 7 inches (17.8 cm) down from the top corner and mark this point with a pin (point A). At the bottom corner of the same side, measure 10 inches (25.4 cm) from the corner across the bottom and pin (point B). Draw a line between the points and pin along the line.

4

Fold the ribbon in half, and insert the folded end of the ribbon between the two scarves just below point A. (To fit a larger bust, you might need to move the folded end a few inches (or centimeters) lower; unfortunately, this involves guesswork, but you'll have a chance to make changes in step 7.) The folded end should be sticking out of what will be the center front seam, by about ½ inch (1.3 cm).

Sizing It Up

The scarves used to make the dress shown here measured 26 inches (66 cm) square, and our model is a size Extra Small/Small. Using scarves 28 inches (71.1 cm) square will net you a size Large/Extra Large.

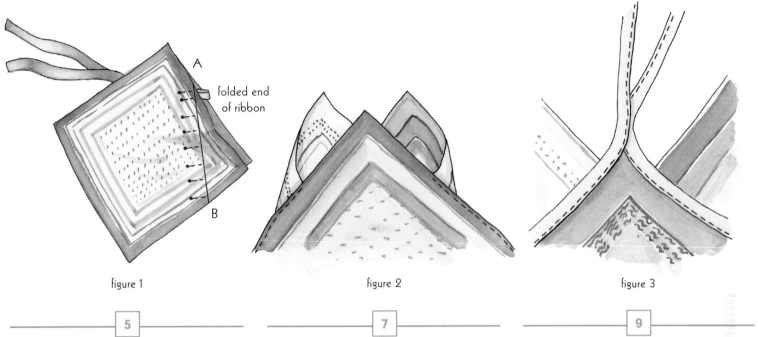

A

folded end
of ribbon

B

figure 1   figure 2   figure 3

5

Stitch the line from point A to point B, catching the folded end of your ribbon in the seam (figure 1). Trim off the excess scarf fabric and press the seam allowance to one side. (Hold off on finishing the seams until after you've checked for size in a later step.)

6

For the side seams and back of the dress, open the front of the dress so the right side faces up. Lay scarf 3 on top of scarf 1 or 2 (it doesn't matter which, because both sides will be treated the same way), with right sides facing. Measure 9 inches (22.9 cm) down from the top corner and mark with a pin. Pin the rest of the way down that side, then stitch. Line up the other side of scarf 3 with the remaining scarf, then mark and stitch in the same way. The result will be three triangle tops, two for the front and one for the back (figure 2).

7

Now's the time to check for fit. You might need help holding up the triangle tops to see how things will work when the finished dress is tied. To make this dress a smaller size, bring the front and side seams up closer to the top; to make a larger size, carefully rip out stitches in those seams to start the seams farther down. This is also your last chance to lower the folded ribbon from step 4, if needed. When you're satisfied, backstitch the tops of all the seams to secure them. Finish the seam allowances with a zigzag stitch, or with a serger if you have one.

8

Measure the front of the dress along the top edge and cut a strip of bias tape to fit. Pin the bias tape to that edge, sandwiching the fabric into the fold of the tape (page 26). Topstitch in place.

9

Fold the remaining bias tape in half, and cut. Fold one of the pieces in half again, and mark the center point. Line up that point with a side seam and pin the bias tape to the top edge as you did for the front. This time there will be extra tape left over in the front and back, for straps. Pin the last bias strip to the other side of the dress.

10

Overlap the bias tape at the center back (figure 3) and topstitch the bias tape from end to end. Tie the shoulder straps to fit, tie the ribbon in back, and you're done!

On the Edge

dress up a t-shirt
by encasing
its edges.

designed by Lily+Amy

What You Do

1

Cut out five rectangles from the scarf. All the pieces should have the same pattern except for the bow center, which could be a contrasting pattern or a solid color from any other part of the scarf. The width and length of the strips you cut may vary depending on your shirt size. In general, this is what you'll need, but measure the hem around the sleeves and neckband to be sure, and adjust as necessary:

• Two strips for the sleeves, 2 x 11 inches (5.1 x 27.9 cm)

• One strip for the collar, 2 x 21 inches (5.1 x 53.3 cm)

• One strip for the bow, 2 x 31 inches (5.1 x 78.7 cm); connect two shorter pieces, if necessary

• One strip for the bow center, 2 x 1½ inches (5.1 x 3.8 cm)

2

Press all the strips as if making double-fold bias tape (page 25). Press the short ends under ¼ inch (6 mm), press the strips in half lengthwise, then press under the long raw edges ¼ inch (6 mm). Stitch the edges together, using a color of thread that will blend in.

3

Starting at the underarm seam, pin the sleeve strips onto the hems of the sleeves, hand gathering them a bit to make soft ruffles. The strips should extend a bit beyond the edges of the sleeves while covering the hems. Where the ends of the strips meet, use a whipstitch (page 22) to join them together.

4

Starting at the back of the neck, attach the neckline strips in the same way. The strips should completely cover the neckband.

5

Tie a bow with the longest strip, giving it uneven tail lengths. Tack the bow in place with a few stitches, then hand sew the finished bow, a bit off center, to the shirt neckline.

What You Need

1 vintage scarf with a central pattern and contrasting border, 26 inches (66 cm) square

1 form-fitting T-shirt in your size

Basic Sewing Kit (page 14)

Garden Club

dress or skirt?
you can wear
it either way.

designed by River Takada-Capel

What You Do

1

Fold the scarf in half and cut along the fold to make two large rectangles. Fold these in half again and cut along the folds to make squares. You should now have four 25-inch (63.5 cm) squares.

2

Layer the squares on top of each other, with the border designs matched up in one corner. To make four curved triangle shapes, cut off the opposite corner, starting just inside the border design and cutting diagonally across the squares at a slight curve (figure 1).

3

Cut the following from the jersey:

- Four rectangular panels, 6 x 25 inches (15.2 x 63.5 cm) wide

- One waist/bust band for your size: Small, 20 x 26 inches (50.8 x 66 cm); Medium, 24 x 30 inches (61 x 76.2 cm); Large, 28 x 34 inches (71.1 x 86.4 cm)

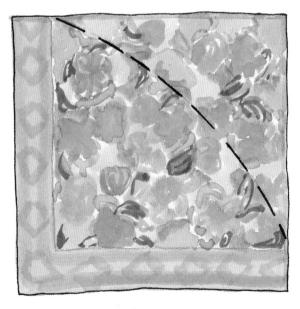

figure 1

What You Need

1 large heavyweight scarf, 50 inches (127 cm) square

1 yard of jersey fabric in a corresponding color

Basic Sewing Kit (page 14)

Finished Sizes
Small, Medium, Large

Seam Allowance
¼ inch (6 mm) unless otherwise noted

4

Fold the waist/bust band in half lengthwise, right sides facing, and serge the short sides together to create a tube. If you don't have a serger, use a wide zigzag stitch. Fold the tube in half in the opposite direction, with the sewn seam on the inside. The folded edge will be the top of the band. Slide it over your hips and bust to make sure it fits. If it needs adjustments, do them now before you move on to the next step.

5

Line up the four triangles and four panels next to each other in an alternating order (scarf, jersey, scarf, jersey). When they're lined up edge to edge, they should create a circle shape with a hole in the center. Stitch the pieces together, right sides facing, one at a time. The knit pieces will touch at the top corner of each scarf piece (figure 2).

6

To add the waist/bust band, you should fold the knit tube in half once, with the seam on the inside. Since this fabric is stretchy, it helps to mark four "corners" of the tube, so you can pin it to your skirt evenly. With the tube laid flat and the sewn seam (which counts as one corner) on one side, mark the opposite fold with a pin. Open up the tube, match the seam and pin together, and lay the tube flat again. Mark the new folds with a pin. The pins (and seam) should now be evenly spaced apart.

7

Slide the folded tube over the skirt so the raw edges line up and right sides are together. Match the pinned "corners" of your tube up to the four corners of the scarf, and pin the two pieces together at these points. Work around the circle, evenly spacing the inside skirt to the tube. Pin as you go and stretch the fabric as needed.

8

Choose a starting point and stitch around the circle. Remove pins before you sew over them, and stretch the fabric where needed so you don't create puckers or unwanted pleats. If you're using a sewing machine, use a wide zigzag stitch and backstitch at both ends. Or if you prefer to use a serger, serge ½ inch (1.3 cm) over your starting point and leave a long thread tail. Tie a knot close to the fabric so the serge doesn't ravel.

9

Use a zigzag stitch on the sewing machine to make a ½-inch (1.3 cm) double-fold hem (page 24) along the bottom of the skirt.

figure 2

Stay Cool

flirty fun for spring
and summer.

designed by River Takada-Capel

What You Need

1 scarf, 42 inches (106.7 cm) square

Ribbon, yarn, or cording for straps
64 inches (162.6 cm) long

Basic Sewing Kit (page 14)

Finished Size
Small to Medium

Seam Allowance
½ inch (1.3 cm) unless otherwise noted

Choosing the Right Scarf

The project shown was made from a large, 100-percent cotton scarf made in India. The feel and drape is so soft, you just want to keep it close to your body—perfect for the summer heat. Try different fibers to see which drape suits you the best. The dress is sewn completely on the bias, so it conforms to any body shape.

What You Do

1

Mount a new needle in the sewing machine and make sure you have enough stabilizer (page 20) on hand for the project.

2

Fold the scarf in half along the bias, right sides together, and match opposite corners to form a triangle. Pin the edges together.

- For the front of the dress, measure 6 inches (15.2 cm) from the top corner. Edgestitch from there all the way to the folded edge. To allow for size adjustments, do not backstitch at the beginning, but do backstitch at the fold.

- For the back of the dress, measure 14 inches (35.6 cm) from the top corner. Without backstitching at the beginning, edgestitch from there all the way to the folded edge; backstitch.

3

Lay the triangle down on a flat surface. Carefully cut a starting point in the bottom fold, at one corner, and then cut along the fold to the opposite corner (figure 1).

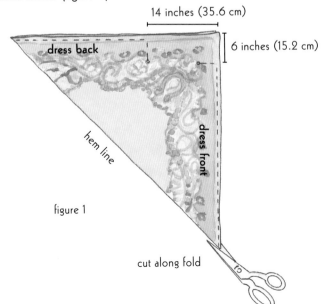

14 inches (35.6 cm)

dress back

6 inches (15.2 cm)

hem line

dress front

figure 1

cut along fold

To finish the hemline, make a ¼-inch (6 mm) double-fold hem (page 24), with either a straight or zigzag stitch. It can be challenging to sew along the bias, and you may opt to leave the seam raw and let it ravel a bit naturally. In that case, a straight stitch ¼ inch (6 mm) from the raw edge will help keep the raveling to a minimum.

5

Leaving the dress wrong side out, open it up and slip it over your head. Pinch the top corners of the dress to hold it up comfortably at your chest, where the straps will be, and look in a mirror. If you want a deeper or shallower V-neckline, mark with fabric chalk where you want to adjust the seam.

6

Check the back in the same way. Make sure the back isn't too low and the dress fits against your body so it isn't loose. If you want to make it tighter or more open, mark where you need to extend the back seam.

7

Slip the dress off and adjust the seams as needed, either extending the stitching or carefully ripping out stitches. You might want to try the dress on again, and when satisfied, backstitch the tops of the seams to secure them.

8

On the dress front, fold under the tips of the top corners by ½ inch (1.3 cm) and hand sew them in place. This creates a narrow casing for the straps.

9

Double the strap material and cut it in half to make two 32-inch (81.3 cm) pieces. Thread one through each of the top casings, and tie knots at the ends of the straps so they don't slide out of the casing.

Breezy

this halter top is
as easy to make
as it is to wear.

◇◇◇◇◇◇◇◇◇◇◇◇◇◇◇◇◇◇◇◇◇◇◇◇

designed by Cathy Landry

What You Do

1

Mount a new needle in the sewing machine and make sure you have enough stabilizer (page 20) on hand for the project.

2

Try on the scarf for fit as described in the Sizing Hints box. Once you know where the top fold needs to be, do the following to make sure the fold is straight:

- Measure down both sides from the top point of the scarf. For instance, 1½ inches (3.8 cm) from the point might be enough, or you might need to measure 2 or 3 inches (5.1 or 7.6 cm) to reach your preferred fold location. Mark the measurement on both sides with tailor's chalk, and fold over the top in a straight line between the marks.

3

Fold the ribbon in half along its length and mark the center with tailor's chalk. Also measure and mark the center of the folded top. Tuck the ribbon into the fold, aligning the marks. Measure about ¼ inch (6 mm) past the edge of the ribbon and cut off the point of the scarf (figure 1).

4

Fold under the cut edge ¼ inch (6 mm) and pin. If you feel the casing is too long, add a few pleats or gathers before edgestitching it in place (figure 2). Stitch through all layers to keep the ribbon from slipping. Press carefully.

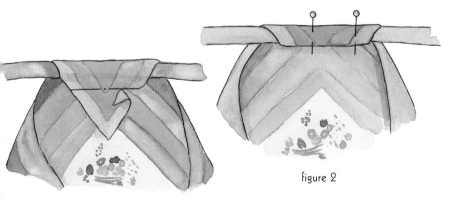

figure 1

figure 2

What You Need

1 square scarf (see Sizing Hints for sizes)

60 inches (1.5 m) of polyester satin ribbon, ⅝ inches (1.6 cm) wide

Basic Sewing Kit (page 14)

Candle and lighter (optional)

Finished Sizes
Small, Medium, Large

Seam Allowance
⅜ inch (1 cm) unless otherwise noted

Sizing Hints

As a general guide, you can go by the dimensions listed below:

- Small, use a 26-inch (66 cm) square scarf
- Medium, use a 28-inch (71.1 cm) square scarf
- Large, use a 30- to 31-inch (76.2–78.8 cm) square scarf

However, fitting the halter top may involve some trial and error. Try this:

- Wrap the scarf around your body with the opposing corners (across the diagonal) in the front, and pin. This will tell you right away if the scarf is large enough.
- Rotate the pinned area to the back. Fold over the top edge in the front as desired, leaving optimal bust coverage. Pin the folded edge.
- Rotate the pins from the back to the front and unpin to remove the scarf. You'll adjust this seam later to make a French seam, so there's no need to mark it now.

5

Carefully and quickly pass the raw ends of the ribbon over a lit candle to singe the edges. Of, if you prefer, fold over each end of the ribbon twice and topstitch in place.

6

To check the fit, tie the ribbon around your neck and pin the opposite corners in the back, wrong sides together (you may need a friend to help you with this step). Carefully remove the halter without removing the pins. Draw a slightly curved seam with tailor's chalk where the seam will be located (figure 3). Since you'll make a French seam (page 26), stitch the seam with wrong sides together. Do not trim off the scarf points yet.

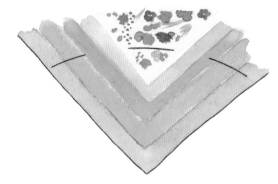

figure 3

7

Try on the halter. Make sure it's not too loose or too tight, keeping in mind that the next step will take an additional ⅜ inch (1 cm). Make any necessary adjustments. Press the seam open to set the seam, then press the seam allowances to one side. Trim the seam allowance to ¼ inch (6 mm). Turn the halter wrong side out, so the right sides are together, with the back seam exactly on the fold. Pin in place and stitch ⅜ inch (1 cm) from the fold to encase the seam allowance. Check the right side to be sure no ravelled threads are showing, and press the seam to one side.

Hits the Spot

slip this on for
instant chic.

designed by Joan Morris

What You Need

1 scarf, approximately 13 x 60 inches (33 x 152.4 cm)

1 lace-edged full slip in your size

Spray starch

Fray retardant

Basic Sewing Kit (page 14)

Seam Allowance
¼ inch (6 mm) unless otherwise noted

◇◇◇◇◇◇◇◇◇◇◇◇◇◇◇◇

Tips for Success

- If your scarf is smaller or a different shape, piece it together as needed to make the strips. It's fine to use two different coordinating scarves to make up the difference. Finish any seams with a small zigzag satin stitch next to the seam then cut off the raw edges.

- If your slip measures more than 44 inches (111.8 cm) around at the hemline, you may need a scarf strip for the hem that is longer than 60 inches (152.4 cm), or you won't have much in the way of gathers. Rule of thumb: the gathering strip should be 1½ to 2 times longer than the fabric edge it's being sewn to.

◇◇◇◇◇◇◇◇◇◇◇◇◇◇◇◇

What You Do

1

Mount a new needle in the sewing machine and make sure you have enough stabilizer (page 20) on hand for the project, if needed.

2

Spray the scarf with spray starch and press, following the manufacturer's instructions. This will make it easier to work with the scarf fabric if it's slippery.

3

Measure and cut the scarf lengthwise to make two strips that are 4 x 60 inches (10.2 x 152.4 cm) and one strip that is 5 x 60 (12.7 x 152.4 cm). Set aside one strip 4 x 60 inches (10.2 x 152.4 cm) with one finished hem for the top of the slip (the yoke); you'll use the other strip of the same size to make the straps; the slightly wider strip will serve for embellishing the hem.

4

Apply fray retardant along any raw edges, following the manufacturer's instructions.

5

For the hem ruffle, stitch the short ends of the hem strip together, right sides facing, to make a circle. The finished seam will be the bottom of the ruffle. Gather the top edge.

figure 1

6

With right sides facing, pin the gathered strip around the slip above the hem lace, with the gathered edge facing down (figure 1). Adjust the gathers evenly and stitch the ruffle in place. Press the gathered strip down over the lace hem.

7

Cut the strap strip in half to make two 4 x 30-inch (10.2 x 76.2 cm) pieces. Make a thin, 1/8-inch (3 mm) single-fold hem (page 24) on both long sides of the strips. Gather one short end of each strip.

8

With right sides facing up, stitch the gathered ends of the straps to the front of the slip, over the top of the slip's original straps. Don't worry about the raw edges showing; they will be covered later. Run the scarf straps over the slip straps to the back. Figure out what length you want, add 1 inch (2.5 cm), and cut the straps. Gather the cut end of each scarf strap, pin them in place to the back, and stitch. Cut off the slip straps underneath the scarf straps

---
9

For the yoke, make a thin, 1/8-inch (3 mm) single-fold hem (page 24) on the raw edge. Fold the strip in half lengthwise to find and mark the center point on the hemmed edge. Pin the center point to the front center of the slip, just below the lace. The scarf strip will be wider than the lace around the top; that will be addressed later. Pin the hemmed edge of the scarf strip all the way around the slip, following the lace line.

10

From the center front to the center back, stitch the yoke to the slip. Starting again at the center front, do the same in the other direction. Where the yoke ends meet in the center back, stitch them together. Make a zigzag satin stitch along the seam and trim off any excess seam allowance.

11

Pin the top edge of the yoke in position at the top of the slip. Where the strap is stitched to the slip, stitch the yoke over the strap at all four points.

12

To make the yoke fit properly, gather it from the top edge to the bottom edge, by hand, at eight locations:

• the centers of all four straps

• both side seams

• center front and center back

After you have made each gathered line, pin it to the slip. Machine stitch along all gathered lines.

13

Hand sew the top of the yoke to the top of the lace.

Bombay Dreams

layer exotic scarves for a boho-chic skirt.

❖❖❖❖❖❖❖❖❖❖❖❖❖❖

designed by Dawn Livera

What You Need

2 scarves (see About the Scarves)

Elastic long enough to encircle your body
above the bustline, ½-inch (1.3 cm) wide

Basic Sewing Kit (page 14)

Finished Size
Adjustable; 39 inches (99 cm) long

Seam Allowance
⅜ inch (9.5 mm) unless otherwise noted

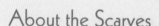

About the Scarves

This dress was made with two *dupatta* scarves, traditionally worn with Indian Punjabi suits. These started
out about 46 x 80 inches (116.8 x 203.2 cm), but the
exact measurements are really not important, since most
of these scarves are easily wide and long enough to make
the dress. Many options are available online as well as
in shops that specialize in Eastern imports. An elaborate
pattern with beading and/or sequins is best for the outside panels. The scarf beneath—the underskirt—can be
fairly plain, but look for a fringed or beaded edging that
will show along the bottom.

What You Do

1

Mount a new needle in the sewing machine and make sure you have enough stabilizer (page 20) on hand for the project.

2

Fold the scarf you've chosen for the underskirt in half, and cut two panels that measure 40 inches (101.6 cm) from the finished bottom edge. If your scarf is 80 inches (203.2 cm) long, you can just cut it in half. Do the same for the outermost panels, but cut them 34 inches (86.4 cm) long.

3

Fold each panel in half across the width and mark the center point of the top (cut) edge with a fabric marker or safety pin.

4

If one of your scarves is wider than the other, hand sew a loose running stitch (page 22) along the top edge of each of the wider panels and evenly gather them to the width of the narrower scarf (figure 1).

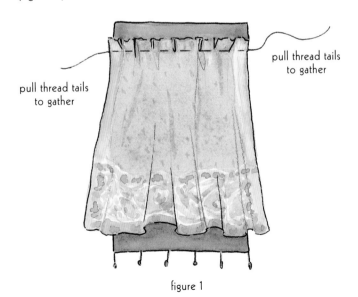

pull thread tails to gather

pull thread tails to gather

figure 1

5

With right sides facing, pin the two underskirt panels together and stitch the side seams. Press the seams open.

6

With the underskirt wrong side out, place one of the outer panels on top of it with the wrong side facing up (figure 2). (This may seem counterintuitive, but things will work out.) Line up the top center marks and side edges, and stitch along the top edge. Repeat with the remaining panel on the other side of the dress.

wrong side out

wrong side up

figure 2

7

Flip the dress right side out, with the outer panels on top (they should be right side facing out). Press the top seam so the underskirt fabric does not show along the top edge. To make the casing, stitch 1 inch (2.5 cm) from the top edge all the way around the dress, leaving an opening for the elastic.

8

Use a safety pin to insert the elastic into the casing (page 24). Put on the dress and adjust the length of the elastic for a comfortable fit. Firmly stitch the ends of the elastic together. Trim off any extra elastic and stitch the casing closed.

Skirting the Issue

If you prefer, wear this as a strapless dress with a wide belt.

Flutters

make a camisole
fabulous by
adding ruffles.

◇◇◇◇◇◇◇◇◇◇◇◇◇◇◇◇◇◇

designed by Joan Morris

What You Do

1

Press and starch the scarf, following the manufacturer's instructions. This will make it easier to cut the slippery fabric.

2

Draw an 8-inch (20.3 cm) circle pattern on scrap paper, using a compass or a plate as a template. Plan where the circle templates will go on the scarf, to make maximum use of interesting colors and patterns. Make sure you leave room to cut out a total of 7 circles. Pin the template in place as needed and cut out the circles.

3

To make the strips, cut the center out of each circle. At the widest point, make them 1½ inches (3.8 cm) wide, tapering to a point at each end (figure 1).

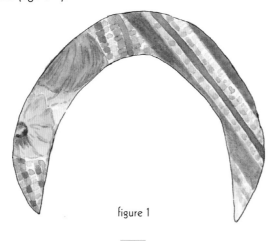

figure 1

4

Apply fray retardant to all raw edges, following the manufacturer's instructions.

What You Need

1 multicolor scarf (see Scarf Size)

Spray starch

Fray retardant

Black satin top in your size

Basic Sewing Kit (page 14)

Compass or dinner-plate template, 8 inches (20.3 cm) in diameter

Scarf Size

You will be cutting seven 8-inch (20.3 cm) circles from the scarf, using either a compass or a dinner plate the right size to make the circle. To have enough fabric, the scarf needs to be at least 26 inches (66 cm) square or 18 x 34 inches (45.7 x 86.4 cm). For the best results, choose a scarf with a lot of variety in pattern and color, preferably with a wide border.

Plan where you want to place six ruffles across the front of the top (save the last ruffle for the neck). On the example, it worked to place a ruffle at each strap, then space the rest about 3 inches (7.6 cm) apart. For each ruffle, place one pointed end of the circle strip at the neckline and stretch out the ruffle with the other end at the hem. Trim the ruffle to fit, as needed, and apply fray retardant on the trimmed edge. Pin the ruffles in place along the inside curve of each circle strip.

6

To sew each ruffle into position, machine stitch a small zigzag satin stitch as close as you can to the edge of the ruffle. Be sure to pull the ruffle tight as you sew, as this will make the ruffle more wavy. Stitch all six ruffles in this fashion.

7

For the neckline ruffle, pin the inside curve of the circle strip along the inside edge of the top, so the ruffle faces up. Use the same zigzag satin stitch to sew it in place.

Double Trouble

you're never too young for style.

◇◇◇◇◇◇◇◇◇◇◇◇◇◇◇◇◇◇◇◇◇

designed by Rachel Le Grand

What You Need

For each skirt, 1 long rectangular scarf, approximately 40 x 11 inches (101.6 x 28 cm)

For each skirt, 24 inches (61 cm) of elastic (or enough to fit the girl's waist), ⅜ inch (9.5 mm) wide

Basic Sewing Kit (page 14)

Finished Size
Adjustable (see Tips for Success)

Seam Allowance
½ inch (1.3 cm) unless otherwise noted

What You Do

1

These instructions make one skirt. Mount a new needle in the sewing machine and make sure you have enough stabilizer (page 20) on hand for the project.

2

If the scarf has any tags, carefully remove them. Fold the scarf in half lengthwise, right sides together, and pin the ends together. Stitch the ends (this will be the side seam of the skirt), taking care to backstitch at the beginning and end of the seam. Press the seam allowances open.

3

To make the casing (page 24), fold under the top edge of the skirt ⅝ inch (1.6 cm) to the wrong side and press. Stitch the edge of the casing all the way around, leaving an opening of about 2 inches (5.1 cm).

4

Use a safety pin to pull the elastic through the casing (page 24). Overlap the elastic ends about 1 inch (2.5 cm), then zigzag stitch the ends together. Slip the elastic into the casing and sew the opening closed by hand or by machine.

Tips for Success

• Your best bet is to use a scarf that's about twice as long as the hip measurement of the little girl you have in mind.

• Take care when ironing the scarf! If the iron's too hot, it could damage the fabric. Read the fiber content on the tag and adjust the iron settings accordingly. No tag? In that case, proceed with caution, starting at a low heat setting and slowly working your way higher.

Flaunt

Whisper
Waisting Time
Labyrinth
Flora
Bon Voyage
Hoppy
Chelsea
Puppy Love
Use Your Head
Knotty
Coquette

Whisper

feather-light and sittin' pretty.

◇◇◇

designed by Casey Dwyer

What You Do

1

Be sure your vintage scarf has been laundered. Press out any wrinkles in the fabric scraps, using an iron on a low setting and using a bit of spray starch (following the manufacturer's instructions) to give the scarf a little more body. Don't forget to use a pressing cloth (page 18).

2

Locate the templates on page 124 and trace them onto heavy cardstock. Cut them out.

3

Decide which parts of your vintage scarf you'd like to use for the earrings. Cut two 6-inch (15.2 cm) squares from the scarf.

4

Place all of the fabric scraps (scarf, felt, cotton, and netting) on top of one another. Place the templates on top of the stack, wherever you find the design appealing. If you feel more comfortable tracing each template onto the fabrics, go ahead, but you might find it easier to hold the template tightly against the stack and cut around it. Cut two stacks of large leaves and two stacks of small leaves. You might not use all these pieces, but not to worry—make a pair for a friend if you've got any left over. The point is, now you have options.

What You Need

1 vintage scarf

Scraps of felt (preferably wool felt), cotton muslin, and tulle/poly netting, each 6 inches (15.2 cm) square

Spray starch (optional)

2 sterling silver S-hook ear wires (the kind that don't require jump rings)

Fray retardant (optional)

Basic Sewing Kit (page 14)

Small scissors with a fine tip

Finished Size
3 inches (7.6 cm) long

5

Use the two large felt leaves as the bases for your earrings; they'll give your earrings some extra stability. Look through the cutouts and stack five to seven pieces on top of the felt bases. Fan them out a bit to show off the details.

6

Using a straight stitch, start at what will be the top of the earrings and stitch a line 1 to 1½ inches (2.5 to 3.8 cm) long directly down the center of the stack. Snip any excess strings.

7

Approximately ⅛ inch (3 mm) from the tops of the earring pieces, snip a tiny hole. It doesn't need to be large; just puncture the pieces enough to slip a straight pin though. Work the straight pin or the scissors' tip through the hole to widen it a little bit (figure 1).

8

Holding the top of an earring with the right side toward you, slip the end of the ear wire into the hole. Work the ear wire through the piece until the earring body sits comfortably in the finding. Repeat for the other earring.

9

If you wish, apply fray retardant around all the edges of your fabric pieces and the ear wire hole, following the manufacturer's instructions.

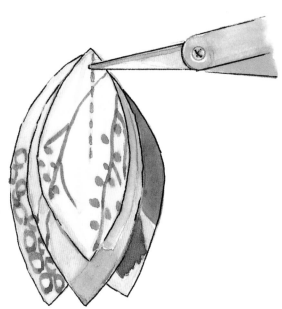

figure 1

Waisting Time

with carefully chosen
fabrics, a reversible
belt can cinch up
twice as many outfits.

designed by Tiffany Laing

What You Need

1 scarf, large enough to fold in thirds and tie around your waist; the one used for this example was 12 x 60 inches (30.5 x 152.4 cm)

Stabilizer (page 20), 9 x 14-inch (22.9 x 35.6 cm) piece

Fusible web, 9 x 14-inch (22.9 x 35.6 cm) piece

2 pieces of fabric (same or contrasting) for front and back of belt panel, each 6 x 14 inches (15.2 x 35.6 cm)

1 yard (91.4 cm) of matching double-fold bias tape, ½ inch (1.3 cm) wide

Fray retardant (optional)

Basic Sewing Kit (page 14)

Craft knife

Cutting mat or cardboard

Felt-tip marker with fine point

Finished Size
With a scarf the right length, this belt can fit any waistline; the shaped front is 13¼ inches (33.7 cm) across

What You Do

1

Mount a new needle in the sewing machine. Enlarge the template on page 124, make two copies, and cut them out around the outside line. Tape the pattern halves together at the wide end, lining up the edges and center line. Use a craft knife and cutting mat to cut out the small rectangular slats.

2

Using the marker, trace the template on both the stabilizer and fusible web. With scissors, cut out two pieces from each material, following the outside edge. Trace the slats but leave them uncut.

3

Place one stabilizer piece on the ironing board with the marked side face down. Place a piece of fusible web on top of it, matching all edges. Lay your fabric of choice, right side up, on top. Cover with a damp pressing cloth. Fuse the layers together, following the manufacturer's instructions. Lift and press the iron, rather than sliding it. Allow to cool, and check to see that the layers have bonded. Press again if needed.

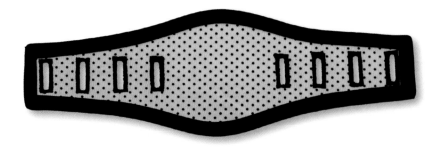

4

Repeat for the second side. With this step complete, you'll have two sides, each made up of bonded fabric, fusible web, and stabilizer. Trim off the excess fabric with scissors, using the stabilizer as a guide. Use your cutting mat and craft knife to cut out the rectangular slats on both pieces.

5

Place one piece, fabric side down, on the ironing board. Place a scrap of fusible web in the center and a few scraps at the ends. Place the remaining piece on top, fabric side up. Press again, as in step 3, to tack the two sides together without having to pin them.

6

Apply bias tape to the belt edge, starting at one of the short sides and mitering the corners as you go (page 26). Overlap the tape ends to finish.

7

Use satin stitch or buttonhole settings to finish the rectangular slats. Trim all thread ends. Apply fray retardant on the front and back of the holes to minimize loosening threads, and allow it to dry. Fold your chosen scarf into thirds, thread it through the slats, and tie it in a knot or bow.

Labyrinth

a clutch perfect
for any occasion.

designed by Kerri Laidlaw

What You Do

1

Mount a new needle in the sewing machine and make sure you have enough stabilizer (page 20) on hand for the project.

2

Cut four 9¾ x 18-inch (24.8 x 45.7 cm) rectangles as follows, saving the leftover scarf fabric to cut the strap later:

- One from each of the scarves

- Two from the interfacing

3

To make a template from the butcher paper, measure 1½ inches (3.8 cm) down from both outside corners and mark. Fold the strip in half, matching the marks. Cut a curved line from the marks to the fold. Unfold the paper to inspect the curved top line (figure 1). Re-cut, if desired, until you're satisfied with the shape.

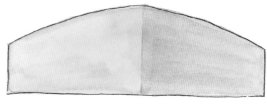

figure 1

4

Pin the two scarf rectangles and the two interfacing rectangles together and pin the paper template to one end. Cut the curve shape into all four pieces at once.

5

Pin the interfacing to the wrong side of each scarf piece and baste around the outside, ⅜ inch (1 cm) from the edge.

What You Need

2 coordinating scarves (for the outside and lining), each measuring at least 9¾ x 18 inches (24.8 x 45.7 cm)

Heavy interfacing (*not* iron-on), 20 x 36 inches (50.8 x 91.4 cm)

Clasp and toggle, 1 inch (2.5 cm) long

Butcher paper for making a template, 4 x 10 inches (10.2 x 25.4 cm)

Basic Sewing Kit (page 14)

Finished Size
Closed: 6 x 9 inches (15.2 x 22.9 cm)

Seam Allowance
½ inch (1.3 cm) unless otherwise noted

6

Fold over the straight, bottom edge of each of the two pieces ½ inch (1.3 cm) and stitch to make hems. Set the pieces aside.

7

Use the remaining scarf fabric to cut two strips for the tie strap as follows:

- One strip 2½ x 14 inches (6.4 x 35.6 cm)
- One strip 2½ x 3 inches (6.4 x 7.6 cm)

8

Fold and press both strips down the center along the length, then press under the sides ½ inch (1.3 cm), as if making double-fold bias tape (page 25). Edgestitch the folded edges together. Set aside.

9

Match up the scarf pieces, right sides facing. Decide which will be the lining and which will be the clutch exterior. Before pinning them together, adjust the hemmed bottom edges so that the lining is slightly lower than the other piece. (This will prevent the lining from showing on the outside.) Pin on the long sides only for now, and do not stitch yet.

figure 2

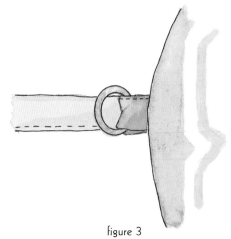

figure 3

10

Thread the short strap piece through the circle portion of the toggle, and fold the strap to make a loop. Match the raw edges up with one raw edge of the long strap (the other half of the toggle will be attached later) and pin them together. Position the two strips between the two scarf fabrics as shown (figure 2). If the long strap has a prettier side that you want facing out, make sure that side is facing the exterior scarf fabric, with the short loop beneath it. Pin along the top of the curve, with the straps between the fabrics.

11

Stitch the three sides together, leaving the hemmed straight edge open. Clip the corners close to the stitching on either side of the curve and turn the fabrics right side out through the opening. The two straps will extend from the center curve (as shown in figure 3). Press.

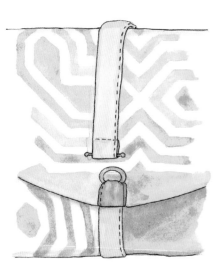

figure 4

12

Pin together the open bottom edges, wrong sides together, and stitch. Two rows of stitching will show on the outside.

13

Fold the straight, bottom edge up (lining inside) about 6 inches (15.2 cm) and pin both sides. Edgestitch.

14

To finish the tie, wrap it around the clutch as shown and test folding under the raw edge enough for the toggle clasp to close (figure 4). When satisfied, stitch the toggle bar into the raw edge. (If you have enough of the strip folded over, you can stitch the end down, tuck the toggle bar into the folded area, and hand sew the bar in place.)

Flora

embellish a plain
scarf to add
flair and drama.

✕✕✕✕✕✕✕✕✕✕✕✕✕✕✕✕

designed by Alice Pino-Marina

What You Do

1

Mount a new needle in the sewing machine and make sure you have enough stabilizer (page 20) on hand for the project.

2

Fold the fabric scrap in half lengthwise, wrong sides together. Stitch the long edges together, backstitching at the beginning and end of the seam. Trim the seam allowance, and turn the fabric inside out to make a tube.

3

Thread the scarf through the tube, and then stitch the two ends of the scarf together. Pull the tube down to cover this seam, and hand sew a few stitches to keep it in place.

4

Wrap the floral appliqué (or doily or jewelry) around the scarf somewhere. I prefer placing it off center. You can tack it in place with a few stitches by hand or by machine.

What You Need

1 vintage scarf, 30 to 40 inches (76.2 to 101.6 cm) long and no more than 12 inches (30.5 cm) wide

Scrap of stretch fabric (T-shirt material, for example), 2 x 3 inches (5.1 x 7.6 cm)

1 floral appliqué, doily, or jewelry of some sort

Basic Sewing Kit (page 14)

Seam Allowance
½ inch (1.3 cm) unless otherwise noted

◇◇◇◇◇◇◇◇◇◇◇◇◇◇◇◇◇◇◇◇

Variety Is the Spice

If the cowl is long enough, you can wrap it around your neck twice for added volume. You can also use a square scarf that is cut into strips and sewn together. Enjoy!

◇◇◇◇◇◇◇◇◇◇◇◇◇◇◇◇◇◇◇◇

Bon Voyage

turn a souvenir into
a cute handbag—
it's a snap

✕✕✕✕✕✕✕✕✕✕✕✕✕✕✕✕

designed by Susan Manthorpe

What You Do

1

Press the fusible interfacing to the wrong side of the scarf, following the manufacturer's instructions.

2

Enlarge the template on page 124 and cut it out. Use it to cut two pieces each from the vintage scarf, lining fabric, and fleece. Transfer the hinge markings to the wrong side of all pieces.

3

Place the two scarf pieces together, right sides facing, and sandwich them between the two pieces of fleece. Pin in place. With the fleece outermost, stitch between the hinge markings down the side and around the bottom to the other side. Turn right side out and press gently.

4

Pin the lining pieces together, right sides facing, and stitch between the hinge markings down the sides, leaving an opening 4¾ inches (12 cm) wide at the bottom.

What You Need

1 vintage scarf, at least 21¾ x 11¾ inches (55.2 x 30 cm)

Fusible interfacing, same size as the scarf (and appropriate weight for your scarf fabric)

Lining fabric, same size as the scarf

Fleece batting, same size as the scarf

Rectangle purse frame with loops, 3 x 6 inches (7.6 x 15.2 cm)

Extra strong fabric glue

1 matching chain strap (any length you like)

Basic Sewing Kit (page 14)

Finished Size
10¼ inches (26 cm) high x 9 inches (22.9 cm) at its widest point

Seam Allowance
⅜ inches (9.5 mm) unless otherwise noted

Design Tip
When cutting out the scarf, pay attention to how the scarf pattern will appear on the bag. In this example, cutting slightly on the diagonal provided a bit of drama, and the building names fit nicely into the corners of the bag.

Tuck the outer bag into the lining, right sides facing. Pin and sew between the hinge markings around the top flaps on both sides of the bag.

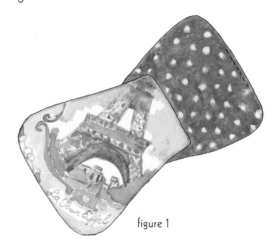

figure 1

6

Carefully pull the outer bag through the opening of the lining. Turn the bag right side out, with the lining still outside the bag (figure 1). Stitch the opening at the bottom of the lining closed. Trim the thread ends and tuck the lining inside the bag. Press the bag gently, paying particular attention to the top and side flap seams.

Open the purse frame, apply a moderate amount of fabric glue around the inside of the frame, and quickly insert the bag flaps into the frame. Be careful not to get excess glue on your bag. Leave overnight to dry.

Attach the chain strap to the loops; *voilà, c'est fini!*

Hoppy

has a favorite winter
scarf gotten worn
out? don't worry—
be Hoppy now.

◇◇◇◇◇◇◇◇◇◇◇◇◇◇◇◇◇◇

designed by Savannah Carroll

What You Need

Fringed wool scarf, 20 inches (50.8 cm) or longer

Heavy weight fusible interfacing, same dimensions as scarf

Felt scraps for the face and ears

2 plastic safety eyes, 12 mm

Embroidery floss for the nose and mouth

1 small bag of polyfill stuffing

Basic Sewing Kit (page 14)

Finished Size
12 inches tall x 5 inches wide at the base (30.5 x 12.7 cm)

Seam Allowance
¼ inch (6 mm) unless otherwise noted

What You Do

1

Enlarge the templates on page 123 and cut them out.

2

Decide which side of the scarf will be the right side, and fuse the fusible interfacing to the wrong side, following the manufacturer's instructions.

3

Fold the fabric in half, right sides together. Place the body pattern on a side with interfacing fused to it and trace around the pattern. Cut through both fabric layers to create two body pieces. Trace and cut two ears and one face from the felt.

4

With all of the pieces right side up, pin the face and ears to one of the body pieces. To achieve the slightly off-center look, allow the right edge of the face piece to overlap the right edge of the body (it will later be enclosed in the seam allowance). Topstitch all three felt pieces to the body, stitching as close as you can to the edges.

Tail Spin

To make the pompom tail:

- Cut about 20 or so fringe strips from the scarf, or cut narrow 2-inch (5.1 cm) strips from the felt.

- Line up the strips and tie them together in the center with embroidery floss.

- Fold the strips at the tie, so all of the ends are bunched together. Wrap the floss around the tied end several times, and tie it off with a knot or two.

- Cut the ends of the strips as desired to shape the tail.

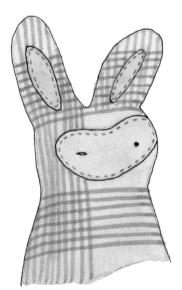

figure 1

5

Decide where you want the safety eyes to be and mark a small dot on the felt for each eye. Cut a small slit on each mark (figure 1). Push the safety eyes through the slits and attach the washers on the wrong side of the fabric to secure the eyes.

6

Lightly draw a nose and mouth on the fabric. Embroider a triangle for the nose shape, and then fill in the triangle with satin stitch (embroidery stitches are described on page 23). Use a backstitch to embroider the mouth.

7

With right sides facing, pin the two body pieces together. Stitch around the edges of the body, leaving an opening 3 inches (7.6 cm) wide at the bottom. Trim or clip the curved seam allowance (page 24).

8

Turn the body right side out through the opening and stuff it with polyfill. Use a point turner to push into the ears and shape the seams. If adding a tail (see box), hand sew it in place with floss before sewing the opening closed.

Chelsea

keep your tresses tidy

designed by Ruth Tower

What You Do

1

Mount a new needle in the sewing machine and make sure you have enough stabilizer (page 20) on hand for the project.

2

Trim the scarf to 9 x 23 inches (22.9 x 58.4 cm).

3

Fold the scarf in half along its length, right sides facing. Stitch the long raw edges together. Turn right side out and press.

4

Use a needle and thread to gather the short end of the scarf in a fan-like shape and secure. Repeat at the opposite edge of the scarf.

5

Thread one gathered end of the scarf through the elastic loop. Fold under the gathered end twice to encase the elastic. Tack down the folded edge by hand, leaving the elastic to rotate freely (figure 1). Repeat at the opposite edge of the scarf.

6

Now stitch the folds securely with a sewing machine. Decorative stitching or thread in a contrasting color can make this connection both strong and attractive. For embellishment, stitch on buttons (or other pretty items such as beads) near the elastic, or any other place you like.

What You Need

1 rectangular scarf, at least 23 inches (58.4 cm) long

1 elastic ponytail holder

2 buttons, ⅝ inch (1.6 cm) in diameter

Basic Sewing Kit (page 14)

Finished Size
4½ x 22 inches (11.4 x 55.9 cm)

Seam Allowance
½ inch (1.3 cm) unless otherwise noted

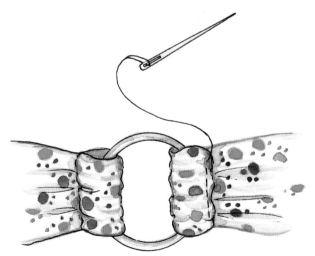

figure 1

Puppy Love

keep close for
constant cuddles.

designed by Cynthia B. Wuller

What You Do

1

To construct the body of the sling:

- Place one flannel piece flat on your work surface with the right side facing up.

- Lay the scarf alongside it, right side up, with the short ends aligned on one side (one end of the scarf will be longer than the flannel). Overlap one long edge of the scarf (on top of the flannel) by ¼ inch (6 mm) and pin.

- Topstitch ⅛ inch (3 mm) from the edge of the scarf.

- Repeat on the other side of scarf with the other piece of cotton (figure 1).

2

Fold the entire stitched piece in half lengthwise, right sides facing. Match up the long edges of the two flannel pieces, pin, and stitch. Open the center seam on the cotton fabric with your fingertip and press it flat. Turn right side out and press the seam again. Lay the sling on a work surface and center the scarf. The cotton edges should be 2¾ inches (7 cm) wide on either side of the scarf. Iron the edges of the cotton fabric flat, keeping the scarf centered.

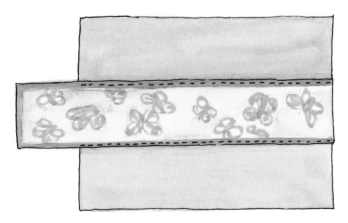

figure 1

1 vintage scarf, 60 x 15½ inches (152.4 x 39.4 cm)

2 pieces of complementary cotton flannel quilting fabric, 49 x 14 inches (124.5 x 35.6 cm)

Basic Sewing Kit (page 14)

Finished Size
Small, but can be adjusted (see Sizing Tip)

Seam Allowance
½ inch (1.3 cm) unless otherwise noted

Sizing Tip

Measure for fit by loosely circling your body with a tape measure, from where your neck and shoulder meet to the top of your waist. About 40 inches (101.6 cm) would be considered size Small, and you can use the measurements provided in these instructions. If your measurement is larger, add the difference beyond 40 inches (101.6 cm) to the *lengths* of the cut pieces.

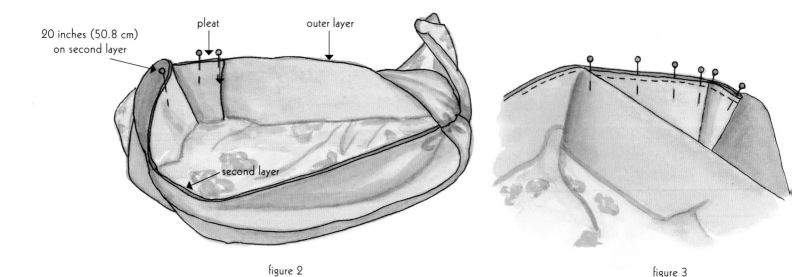

20 inches (50.8 cm) on second layer

pleat

outer layer

second layer

figure 2

figure 3

3

To stitch and gather the shoulder:

- Lay the sling out flat on the work surface. Fold the scarf overhang toward the center, right sides facing, lining up the fold with the edge of the sling.

- Bring the opposite end of the sling over to pin the short ends together, right sides facing, with the scarf overhang between the two ends.

- Stitch the ends with a basting stitch and a ⅜-inch (9.5 mm) seam allowance. Do not backstitch, and leave about 3 inches (7.6 cm) of excess thread on each end of the seam. Pull the bobbin thread on both sides to gather the seam (page 25) to 8 inches (20.3 cm).

- Using a regular stitch length, stitch the gathered seam with a ½-inch (1.3 cm) seam allowance. Stitch again right next to the seam line to reinforce it.

- Turn the sling right side out. Fold the gathered seam in half, wrong sides together, and whipstitch the edges closed ½ inch (1.3 cm) on either side of the seam.

4

Lay the sling on the work surface with the opening facing up and the scarf overhang on the right side. On the outer layer of the sling, measure 15½ inches (39.4 cm) from the shoulder seam and mark it with a pin. Measure ½ inches (1.3 cm) to the left of the pin and mark it with another pin. Make a pleat by folding the fabric to the inside on the first pin, and back in the other direction on the second pin.

5

On the second layer of the sling, measure 20 inches (50.8 cm) from the shoulder seam and mark it with a pin. Fold the fabric so the pin butts up to the edge of the first pleat, and pin it in place (figure 2).

6

Measure 4¾ inches (12 cm) to the left of the last basted pin and pin the three layers together. Fold the second layer of fabric to the right on the last pin, and pin the third and fourth layers together for 3 inches (7.6 cm) past the fold. Edgestitch the pinned areas on both sides of the folded second layer (figure 3). Stitch a second time to reinforce.

7

To wear the sling, put it on with the scarf overhang on your right shoulder and the pouch facing out. You can carry a pet that weighs up to 6 pounds (2.7 kg) in the pouch. Use one hand to support your animal pal while it's in the pouch, especially if it's a very active little critter.

Use Your Head

warm in winter,
cool year 'round.

◇◇◇◇◇◇◇◇◇◇◇◇◇◇◇◇◇◇◇

designed by Joan Morris

What You Need

1 plaid wool scarf, at least 18 x 30 inches (45.7 x 76.2 cm)

1 complementary plaid wool scarf with a smaller check, at least 28 inches (71.1 cm) long

½ yard (45.7 cm) of lightweight sew-in interfacing

½ yard (45.7 cm) of lining fabric

¾ yard (68.6 cm) of grosgrain ribbon, ⅞ inch (2.2 cm) wide

1 button 1¼ inch (3.2 cm) in diameter

Basic Sewing Kit (page 14)

Finished Size
Medium

Seam Allowance
⅝ inch (1.6 cm) unless otherwise noted

What You Do

1

Enlarge the pattern pieces on page 122 and cut them out.

2

Cut out the following pieces:

- From the first scarf (folded in half), pin and cut all the pattern pieces (two of each), except for the band.

- From the interfacing, cut the same pieces as from the scarf.

- From the lining, cut two tops and two sides.

- From the second scarf, cut 2 band pieces on the bias, to give them a little bit of stretch.

3

Pin each interfacing piece to the wrong side of each matching scarf piece and baste ½ inch (1.3 cm) from the raw edges, all the way around. Only one of the visor pieces will have interfacing.

4

Pin the top pieces, right sides facing, along the outside (longer) curve, and stitch. Press the seam open and topstitch ¼ inch (6 mm) from the center seam.

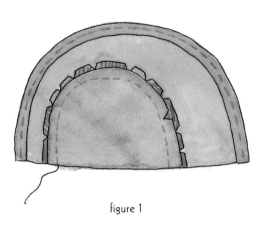

figure 1

figure 2

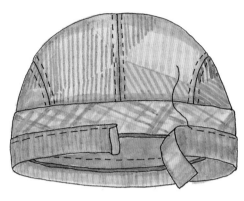

figure 3

5

Pin the side pieces in place along the inside curves. Clip the curves as needed to make the two fit together (figure 1). Stitch, press the seams open, and topstitch ¼ inch (6 mm) from the center seam.

6

Make the lining in the same way (repeat steps 4 and 5), but without the topstitching. With wrong sides together, place the lining inside the cap, match the seams, and pin. Baste close to the edge.

7

With right sides facing, pin the two band pieces together. Starting on the short, flat end, stitch up the short side and all the way across the long top edge, around the point to the inside slit (figure 2). Turn the band right side out and press flat. Baste the raw edges together.

8

With right sides facing, pin the visor pieces together. Leaving ½ inch (1.3 cm) unsewn at both ends, stitch the pieces together along the outside curve. Clip the curves, turn right side out, and press. Baste the raw edge.

9

Fold the remaining bias tape in half, and cut. Fold one of the pieces in half again, and mark the center point. Line up that point with a side seam and pin the bias tape to the top edge as you did for the front. This time, there will be extra tape left over in the front and back, for straps. Pin the last bias strip to the other side of the dress.

10

Pin the visor to the cap, centered in the front, with the raw edges matching. Baste in position.

11

Pin the ribbon to the lower edge of the cap, starting at the center back of the cap, placing one edge slightly over the seam line. Fold under one short edge and overlap the remaining end. Stitch along the seam line (figure 3). Turn the ribbon to the inside, press, and hand sew in place.

12

Hand sew the button in position on the point of the band.

Knotty

this necklace has it
all tied up.

designed by Marilyn Saqqal

What You Do

1

Mount a new needle in the sewing machine and make sure you have enough stabilizer (page 20) on hand for the project.

2

Cut a strip of fabric 4¾ x 60 inches (12 x 152.4 cm) from the scarf. This width, when sewn, will fit around 1-inch (25 mm) beads and give you plenty of length to tie the necklace and shorten if desired. If you're using beads of a different size, adjust the width accordingly. You'll want them to fit snugly inside the scarf tube (see step 3).

3

To make a tube for the beads, fold and pin the fabric strip along its length, right sides facing, and stitch. Check the fit by sliding a bead into the tube and adjust as needed. Remove the test bead.

4

To turn the tube right side out, attach a large safety pin to one end of the tube and push it through the tube to the other end. Remove the safety pin.

What You Need

1 scarf at least 60 inches (152.4 cm) long

10 wooden beads, 1 inch (25 mm) or any size you like

Basic Sewing Kit (page 14)

Seam Allowance
¼ inch (6 mm) unless otherwise noted

Make a tight knot in the center of the tube. With the seam always facing down, insert a bead into the tube and push it tightly against the center knot. Holding the bead in place, make a knot on the other side of the bead, leaving no fabric between the inserted bead and the new knot.

6

Repeat step 5 for the remaining beads, with an even number of beads on both sides of the center knot. Once all the beads are in place, you should have 9 to 12 inches (22.9 to 30.5 cm) of fabric left on each side of the beads. Adjust according to your preference.

To finish the ends of the tube, fold under ½ inch (1.3 cm) of fabric and topstitch closed.

Coquette

it's always fashionable
to catch someone's eye.

designed by Judit Wild

What You Do

1

Cut out a circle 5¼ inches (13.3 cm) in diameter from the scarf, using a bowl, plate, or circle template.

2

To form the yo-yo for the flower, hand sew a running stitch around the perimeter of the circle, close to the edge (figure 1). When you get back to the beginning, pull the thread tight to gather the fabric then tie a knot.

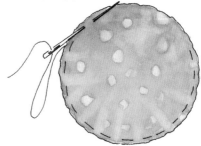

figure 1

3

Put a glass bead on the head pin. Push the pin through the center of the flat side of the yo-yo flower, and then through the gathered center on the other side. Put the bead cap on the other end of the head pin and push all the fabric into the bead cap. Cut off most of the pin with the wire cutter, leaving enough to make a loop (figure 2).

figure 2

4

Link the remaining seven glass beads as follows:

• Slip one glass bead onto an eye pin and cut most of the pin with the wire cutter, leaving enough to make a loop (but don't make the loop yet). Do the same with all of the beads.

• Using pliers, link the beads to each other, one at a time, making the second loop as you go (figure 3).

• When you get to the last bead, link it to the loop on the flower's bead cap and secure.

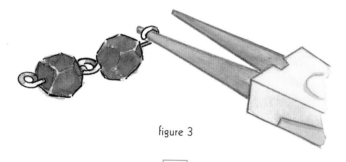

figure 3

5

Cut the chain roughly in half, so you have a 7-inch (17.8 cm) length and an 8-inch (20.3 cm) length. Attach the shorter one to the end of the beads, and attach the longer one to the back loop of the flower.

6

Add the jump rings and the clasps to the end of the chains.

What You Need

1 silk scarf or scarf scrap no smaller than 6 inches (15.2 cm) square

8 black faceted glass beads

1 brass head pin

1 brass-colored bead cap

7 brass eye pins

1 brass chain, 15 inches (38.1 cm) long

2 brass jump rings

1 brass lobster claw clasp

Basic Sewing Kit (page 14)

Bowl or circle template with a diameter of 5¼ inches (13.3 cm)

Round-nose pliers

Wire cutter

Finished Size
17 inches (43.2 cm) long

Decorate

Four Square

Mosaic

Hang It Up

Kashmir

Ring Around the Napkins

In the Shade

Bloom

Flicker

Charmed

Four Square

sewing these
window panels is
a breeze!

designed by Cathy Landry

What You Do

1

Mount a new needle in the sewing machine and make sure you have enough stabilizer (page 20) on hand for the project.

2

On a large, flat surface, arrange the scarves in the order you like best. For neat, finished seam allowances, French seams are recommended (page 26). Starting at the top, pin the first two scarves *wrong* sides together along one edge. Sew ⅜ inch (9.5 mm) from the edge on the *right* side of the fabric.

3

Stitch scarf 2 to scarf 3, then scarf 3 to scarf 4 in the same way. Stitch the second curtain in the same way as the first.

4

Press open all seams, then press them towards one side. Trim each seam allowance to ⅛ inch (3 mm). Fold each seam with *right* sides together, with the stitching line exactly on the fold. Pin in place. Stitch ¼ inch (6 mm) from the fold to encase the raw edge.

5

Check the right side to be sure no ravelled threads are showing. Press the seam allowance to one side. Use four drapery clips along the top edge of each curtain to hang them.

What You Need

8 coordinating square scarves, all the same dimensions

8 drapery clips

Basic Sewing Kit (page 14)

Finished Size
19½ x 75 inches (49.5 x 190.5 cm)

Mosaic

this gorgeous
reversible lap
quilt is sure
to become
an heirloom.

designed by Lisa Schiffleger

What You Do

1

To make the side composed of squares, cut one hundred 5-inch (12.7 cm) squares from a variety of selected fabrics. Lay them out on a flat surface, 10 squares in 10 rows, to set up the design for the top.

2

Starting with the top row, stitch the squares together one at a time, right sides facing, all the way across the row. Press the seams to one side and lay the stitched row back in its place. Do the same with the second row, and so on, until you have 10 stitched rows.

3

Pin the first two rows together, right sides facing, matching up the squares at each seam. Stitch them together, removing pins as you go and backstitching over each seam for reinforcement. Pin and stitch row 2 to row 3 in the same way. Continue until all rows are stitched together, then press the seams.

What You Need

At least 4 yards (3.7 m) of a variety of scarves and fabrics (see Scrounging for Fabric)

2 yards (1.8 m) of batting, preferably cotton or an 80/20 blend

Basic Sewing Kit (page 14)

Finished Size
45 inches (114.3 cm) square

Seam Allowance
½ inch (1.3 cm) unless otherwise noted

◇◇◇◇◇◇◇◇◇◇◇◇◇◇◇◇◇◇◇◇◇

Scrounging for Fabric

You will need at least four or five lightweight wool or wool/acrylic-blend scarves and shawls, depending on their sizes. You can also cut fabric squares from thrift shop finds such as skirts and slacks; just look for fabrics that are all about the same weight. In the example, one side features a central scarf that is at least 29 inches (73.7 cm) square.

◇◇◇◇◇◇◇◇◇◇◇◇◇◇◇◇

4

To make the other side, follow the diagram (figure 1). Feel free to make whatever adjustments to the design that you like, just make sure that the finished size is the same as the other side of the quilt.

- For the central scarf, trim any fringe or hem and be sure it is squared up. This is best done with a rotary cutter, mat, and ruler (page 15).

- Stitch the 6-inch (15.2 cm) side borders first, right sides facing, followed by the same size border above and below.

- Stitch the outside top and bottom borders, followed by the side borders.

- Press all seams.

5

To assemble the quilt:

- Cut the batting slightly larger than the quilt back.

- Fold one side of the quilt into quarters to find the center, and mark it with a safety pin. Do the same with the opposite side and the batting.

- Lay one quilt side on a flat surface, wrong side up. Lay the batting on top of it, matching centers. Lay the opposite side on top, wrong side down, matching centers. Use one safety pin to pin all three layers together.

- Starting from the center and moving toward the sides, pin all layers together in several places. Take care not to stretch the fabrics or allow any of the layers to bunch up.

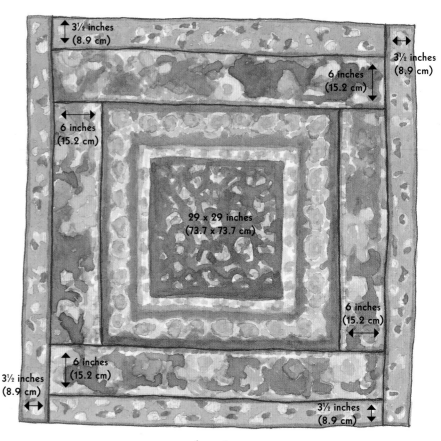

3½ inches (8.9 cm)

3½ inches (8.9 cm)

6 inches (15.2 cm)

6 inches (15.2 cm)

29 x 29 inches (73.7 x 73.7 cm)

6 inches (15.2 cm)

6 inches (15.2 cm)

3½ inches (8.9 cm)

3½ inches (8.9 cm)

figure 1

6

Quilt the layers. This particular quilt has been stitched with the free-motion quilting method (see page 103), but use any method you are comfortable with.

7

When the quilting is done, lay the quilt out on a table and square it up. Trim off the excess batting and backing.

8

Cut fabric strips 2½ inches (6.4 cm) wide and stitch them together to make one long strip at least 5¼ yards (4.8 m) long. Iron them so as to make wide double-fold binding (page 25) and attach the binding to the quilt, mitering the corners (page 26).

Free-Motion Quilting

If you are new to machine quilting, you can search the Internet for easy tips and videos about machine stitch quilting and free-motion quilting. Here are a few pointers to get you started.

Machine Settings

- Drop the feed dogs.

- Put in a new, size 90 needle.

- Attach the darning foot.

- Set the stitch length to -0-.

- Center the needle (if your machine has that option).

- Set the needle to stop in the down position (if your machine has that option).

- Set the sewing speed to medium.

- You may have to decrease your tension.

Other Tips

- Fill at least 3 to 4 bobbins before starting.

- Use standard sewing thread, either cotton or polyester.

- Wearing quilting gloves or rubber fingers will help you grip the quilt as you move it.

- Cut your teeth on a 20 x 20-inch (50.8 x 50.8 cm) scrap the same thickness as the quilt. Get comfortable with moving the fabric at a slow, steady, even pace and check that your settings are good.

- Start in the center of the quilt and work out, especially if you have borders on the top or back of your quilt.

- Quilt a small area at a time, removing the safety pins as you go.

- As you complete small areas, remove the quilt from the machine and straighten/pin the layers as needed.

- All of your hard work will be enhanced by machine washing your quilt on a gentle cycle, then machine drying it. Drying makes the batting shrink a bit, causing the puckered effect that will make your quilting stitches just pop.

Hang It Up

keep your baubles
neat and
organized on a
mod jewelry caddy.

◇◇◇◇◇◇◇◇◇◇◇◇◇◇◇◇◇◇◇◇

designed by Beth Walker

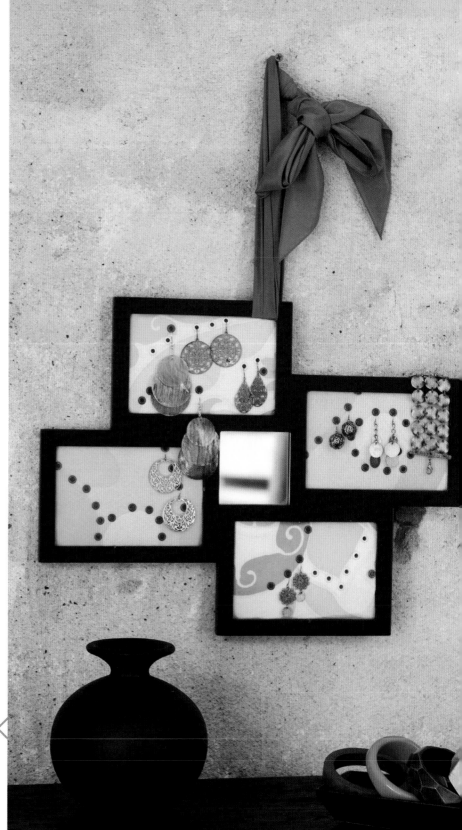

What You Do

1

Lay out a piece of interfacing, non-adhesive side facing up, large enough to accommodate the frame. Remove any glass or backing, and lay the frame on the interfacing. Trace the *outside* of the frame onto the interfacing. Remove the frame and cut along the lines. For a frame with multiple openings, cut a separate piece for each one.

2

Select a retro scarf and decide what parts you want to use. Gently press the scarf, using a damp pressing cloth. Cut the scarf to the size of the interfacing and fuse them together, following the manufacturer's instructions.

Hints for Success

- **Frame:** Keep your eye open for unusual shapes and sizes. The instructions can be adapted for any frame.

- **Eyelets:** These are essentially mini-grommets; this project uses the $5/32$-inch (4mm) size sold in fabric stores. The scrapbooking supplies aisle of your favorite craft store will yield a bonanza of eyelet and grommet types that you can also use: neon colors, silver and gold, and a range of shapes, including squares. Select colors that complement the scarf. In addition to setting tools, keep a screwdriver on hand to remove any eyelets that are poorly hammered.

- **Staple gun:** Be sure to use the listed size of small staples, or you risk splitting the wood on the frame.

- **S-hooks:** Choose ones that have larger openings. If the hooks are like a closed figure 8, they are hard to get into the eyelets. Or, find alternatives such as Christmas ornament hangers, or make your own out of wire.

- **Your workspace:** Make sure you have a protected surface and a place to hammer the eyelets. This could be as simple as a plastic placemat on top of your cutting mat.

What You Need

(For more information on materials, see Hints for Success)

1 scarf large enough to fill the frame opening(s)

Vintage or new frame

Heavy weight fusible interfacing, the thicker the better

Basic Sewing Kit (page 14)

Eyelets, enough to suit you

Hammer and setting tools for eyelets

Staple gun (for large frames), with $5/16$-inch (8 mm) staples

Glue gun or tack tape and clamps (for small frames)

S-hooks, ¾ inch (1.9 cm)

3

Lay the stiffened scarf on a protected flat surface, right side up, and center the frame over it. Position the eyelets on the fabric in a pattern that complements the scarf design, and mark their placement with a dot. At each mark, use scissors to cut a tiny X that will accept the eyelets. **Note:** It's important to first experiment with a fused scarf scrap to make sure the snips of your X aren't too long. Start with tiny cuts, check to see if you can insert the eyelet—it should be a snug fit—and only if it won't fit through should you make the cut a smidge longer.

Insert and set the eyelets. (If you don't want to use eyelets, or inadvertently cut too large an X, consider embroidering the edges of the holes instead.)

4

Lay the frame right side down, so you can access the back. Place the stiffened fabric over the frame, scarf side down. Press the fabric into the frame.

- If using a staple gun, staple around the edges of the frame until the scarf is secure.

- If using glue or strong tape, clamp the fabric on one side of the frame. On the opposite side, apply glue or tape, press the fabric into place, then clamp it.

5

Use a blade or scissors to trim away the fabric edges that stick up beyond the edges of the frame.

6

Hang the frame with wire, as you would any frame, or slip a coordinating scarf around one edge of the frame, working it between staples, and use it as the hanger.

7

Hook earrings can be hung directly into the openings. To hang other types of jewelry, slip S-hooks into the eyelet openings and you're good to go. You can drape necklaces, bracelets, clip earrings, and rings; feel free to stab pins directly into the fabric as needed.

Kashmir

trim your windows
with a kaleidoscope
of color.

designed by Amanda Carestio

What You Need

1 scarf, approximately 28 inches (71.1 cm) square

¾ yard (68.6 cm) of felt, 54 inches (137.2 cm) wide

Glue stick (optional)

Bias piping in a coordinating color, enough to go around each panel, about 5 yards (4.6 m)

4 grommets, ⅜ inch (1 cm), and a grommet setter

Basic Sewing Kit (page 14)

Finished Size

Each panel measures 12½ x 19 inches (31.8 x 48.3 cm)

Hang It Up

There are so many possibilities for hanging mechanisms. You might make hangers for the panels by using leftover fabric, or you could re-purpose a few ball chains. A few pieces of ribbon in a contrasting color and tied with a bow would be pretty, too. You could even hang the panels from clips, and save yourself the trouble of installing grommets.

What You Do

1

Create a template for your particular scarf design, either by copying half of the scarf on a copy machine or by laying the scarf and a piece of paper over a light box and tracing the design. You can make the template any size, as long as you'll be able to cut it from your scarf twice. Or enlarge the template on page 123 and cut out the shaped openings in the template.

2

Cut the felt into four rectangles, each measuring 24 x 13½ inches (61 x 34.3 cm). Place the template on each piece of felt, one at a time, and tape it on the outside edges. Trace all of the interior edges onto the felt with a marker. **Important**: Trace the template face up on two of the pieces and face down on the other two.

3

Cut out all the interior shapes and the outside edges from the felt.

4

Cut the scarf in half and lay one of the halves flat on a table. Apply glue to the back of the felt and position it on top of the scarf half. Press firmly. Let the glue dry for a few minutes and then add some pins for stability.

5

Carefully turn over both the scarf and the felt layer, so the scarf is now on top. Apply glue to the back of the matching felt piece and place it on top of the scarf, matching it up as best you can with the other felt piece. The scarf will be sandwiched between the two felt cutout shapes. Add more pins for stability.

6

Once the glue has dried, stitch around the interior cutout shapes, leaving the outside edges of the felt unstitched. There are lots of curves and turns to make, so use a small stitch length and work slowly. Stitch a second line ¼ inch (6 mm) outside the first stitch line. Both threads can be colors that contrast with the felt (orange and brown were used in the project shown here).

7

If the scarf extends past the edges of the felt shapes, cut off the excess now. Slightly round the corners of the rectangle. Insert the piping between the front and back felt layers, and pin it in place as you work. Topstitch the piping in place.

8

To place the grommets, cut two small holes 1½ inch (3.8 cm) from the left and right edges at the top of the panel. Insert the grommets and set them.

Ring Around the Napkins

would you
have believed
macramé
could look this
dressed up?

designed by Joan Morris

What You Do

What You Need

Assorted scarves

2 ⅓ yards (2.1 m) of cord per napkin ring, ⅜ inch (9.5 mm) in diameter

Fray retardant

Basic Sewing Kit (page 14)

Finished Size
Each, 2½–3 inches (6.4 to 7.6 cm) across

Seam Allowance
½ inch (1.3 cm) unless otherwise noted

1

Mount a new needle in the sewing machine and make sure you have enough stabilizer (page 20) on hand for the project. The primary instructions below are for the napkin ring with a bead. For the alternate design, see Other Knot Designs (page 110).

2

For each napkin ring, cut two pieces of cord, one 60 inches (152.4 cm) long, and one 36 inches (91.4 cm) long.

3

Cut the scarves into strips that are 2 inches (5.1 cm) wide. Stitch the strips together as needed, at the short ends, to make one 60-inch (152.4 cm) long strip and one strip 36 inches (91.4 cm) long for each napkin ring. To add visual interest, make the two strips from two different scarves.

4

Fold each strip along its length, right sides together, and pin. Stitch the entire length, leaving the ends open.

5

Turn the strips while inserting the cording, as follows:

- Match up a strip and cord of the same length.

- Stick a safety pin through one end of the cord and also one end of the fabric tube.

- Slide the safety pin inside the tube, taking the cord with it, through the whole length of the tube.

6

Fold each short cord in half and stitch 1 inch (2.5 cm) down from the fold, catching both cords.

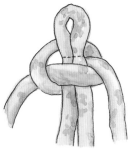

figure 1   figure 2

7

Fold the longer cord in half to find the middle, and place the fold behind the shorter cord at the stitching. Tie the longer cord around the shorter cord in a square knot, with the right-hand cord in front (figure 1). Pull the cords to make the knot snug then tie another knot with the left-hand cord in front. Continue tying knots down the cord, alternating left and right cord in the same way. It may help to hook the short cord loop around something stationary as you tie the knots.

8

When the knotted cording is about 6 inches (15.2 cm) long, stitch the outside cords as close as you can to the end of the macramé (figure 2). Cut the cord 1 inch (2.5 cm) from the stitching. Push the fabric back to expose the cord, and cut the cord at the stitch line. Wrap the ends around to the back, fold them under, and hand sew the ends in place.

9

To finish the center cords:

- Stitch close to the bottom of the square knots, push the fabric back, and cut the cords as before.

- Tuck the ends through the loops at the other ends of the knots.

- Run the ends through a large wooden bead and push the bead up to the loop.

- Tie knots in the end of each scarf cord. Cut the ends off at an angle about 1 inch (2.5 cm) from the knots.

- Apply fray retardant on the ends of the scarf, following the manu-facturer's instructions.

Other Knot Designs

For a variation of the knot explained at left, leave a 1-inch (2.5 cm) space between the square knots. This allows more of the short center cords to show. For a different finish without beads, run the two center cords through the starting loop and hand sew them in place to make a solid ring.

Another option is to make a series of Josephine knots. Use only one scarf-covered cord, 60 inches (152.4 cm) long, and follow the diagram (figure 3). Start with one knot in the center of the cord, and then space the next knot about 1 inch (2.5 cm) away. You can place some of the knots closer as well. Tie knots until the piece is about 8 inches (20.3 cm) long. Run the two ends through the first knot and hand sew them in place on the wrong side of the ring.

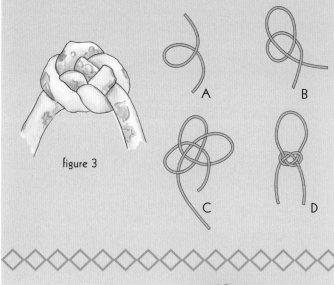

figure 3

In the Shade

plain shades are
a dime a dozen.
jazz it up!

designed by Nathalie Mornu

What You Need

1 scarf, see Bigger is Better

Scrap tissue paper

Drum shade

Craft sticks or disposable palette knife

6 yards (5.5 m) of double-fold bias tape quilt binding

Tape

½ yard (45.7 cm) of fabric

Basic Sewing Kit (page 14)

Craft knife

Hot glue gun and glue sticks

15 bulldog clips or clothespins

Bigger Is Better

You'll need enough material to go around the shade at least twice, plus extra for the embellishment. In the example shown, the shade measures 22 inches (55.9 cm) in diameter, which is about 70½ inches (179.1 cm) in circumference, and 13 inches (33 cm) tall. The scarf measured 64 x 42 inches (162.6 x 106.7 cm). The designer factored in an allowance of 1 inch (2.5 cm) at both top and bottom, and cut two strips each 64 x 15 inches (162.6 x 38.1 cm), leaving some leftover fabric to embellish the top edge of the shade.

What You Do

Prep

---1---

Carefully cut away any materials on the exterior of the shade. Don't remove the lining or any existing materials glued to the top or the bottom of the frame.

---2---

Measure the circumference of the larger end of the shade. Measure the shade from top to bottom and add 1½ inches (3.8 cm). Using these measurements, draw a rectangle on scrap paper. Cut it out, pin it to the scarf, and cut out that rectangle of fabric. Cut out a second rectangle the same size.

---3---

Each rectangle cut in step 2 will cover half the shade, leaving plenty of fabric to make decorative gathers. Use clips to attach one rectangle along the top half of the shade, gathering it decoratively at evenly spaced intervals and with ¾ inch (1.9 cm) of scarf fabric turned inside along the top (figure 1).

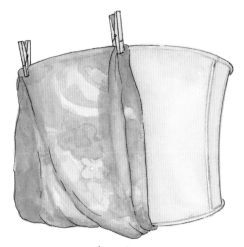

figure 1

4

Pin the lining pieces together, right sides facing, and stitch between the hinge markings down the sides, leaving an opening 4¾ inches (12 cm) wide at the bottom.

5

Turn the lampshade with the clipped edge down, against the work surface. As was done in the previous step, clip the scarf fabric to what is now the upper edge of the shade, gathering it opposite the already clipped and evenly spaced gathers. As you work, pull the scarf fabric taut.

6

Repeat steps 4 and 5 to clip the other rectangle of scarf fabric cut in step 2 to the remaining area of uncovered lampshade. Hide the raw edges of the sides in some pleats.

Fabric Flowers

Determine how many flowers you want to make to decorate the bottom edge of the shade. For each, cut a rectangle that's 4 x 10 inches (10.2 x 25.4 cm). Note: You can vary the size of the rectangle somewhat to make the flowers different sizes and add visual interest. Fold the rectangle in half lengthwise. Roll up the folded rectangle on itself, along its length, as if you were rolling up a sleeping bag, hand stitching it at points along the raw edge so that it stays rolled. Knot the thread and cut off any extra. Use hot glue to attach the flowers to the bottom edge of the shade.

Glue

1

Plug in the hot glue gun. Hot glue the scarf rectangles to the upper edge of the shade, pulling the fabric taut and working in small sections so that before the glue hardens, you can press the glue into the fabric with a craft stick or palette knife to get good adhesion.

2

Allow the glue to harden completely before flipping the shade so the unglued edge faces up. Hot glue the scarf fabric to the shade's edge; as before, pull the fabric taut, work in small sections, and press the glue in with a craft stick. Allow the glue to harden.

3

Carefully clip off any extra fabric on the *inner* edges at the top and bottom of the shade.

4

To cover up the raw edges, hot glue the binding strip along the top and bottom of the shade, catching both the exterior and the interior in its fold.

5

Cut a strip of scarf fabric a little longer than the upper circumference of the shade, twist it tightly, clamp it to the upper edge, then hot glue it down into place.

Bloom

this bouquet
will never wilt.

designed by Joan Morris

What You Do

For the Multicolor Rose

1

Cut two 2 x 20-inch (5.1 x 50.8 cm) strips, each from a different scarf, and cut one 4 x 20-inch (10.2 x 50.8 cm) strip from the tulle.

2

Fold the tulle piece in half lengthwise, so it matches the size of the other strips. Stack the strips, right sides facing up, with a scarf piece on the bottom, folded tulle in the middle, and the remaining scarf on top. The long sides with all the raw edges will be the top of the rose.

3

Along the side with the folded tulle edge, machine baste the three strips together, leaving long thread tails. Fold under the short ends and stitch them to make narrow, single-fold hems. Then use the long thread tails to gather the long edge fairly tightly.

4

Fold over one end of the 16-gauge wire by 1 inch (2.5 cm). Tuck the folded end into one end of the gathered strips. Roll the fabric around the wire to gather it into a flower shape, and hand sew it onto the wire. Don't worry too much about neatness, as the stitches will be covered in the next step. Use pliers to bend and shape the wire as needed to form the stem.

What You Need

Assorted scarves in floral colors, with at least one with green, for leaves

Scraps of tulle (netting)

18 inches (45.7 cm) of wire per flower stem, 16 gauge

Green floral tape, 1/2 inch (1.3 cm) wide

Fusible web

4 inches (10.2 cm) of wire per flower with button center, 24 gauge

Assorted small, round buttons

3-inch (7.6 cm) square scrap of pink felt for rose pin

1¼ inch (3.2 cm) pin back for rose pin

Basic Sewing Kit (page 14)

Wire cutters

Hole punch

Pliers

Finished Size
Each flower, about 4 inches (10.2 cm) across; stem length, 11–13 inches (30–33 cm)

Seam Allowance
½ inch (1.3 cm) unless otherwise noted

5

Cut a piece of floral tape 18 inches (45.7 cm) long. Start wrapping the floral tape around the flower base, pulling the tape tightly (the adhesive in the tape makes it stick to itself). When the base looks finished, with all the rough ends covered, continue wrapping the tape down the wire. Angle the tape and spin the stem as you go, overlapping the tape edges. Wrap the tape all the way down the stem.

6

To make the leaves, use an iron to press fusible web to the wrong side of a green section of scarf; follow the manufacturer's instructions. Draw a leaf shape on the web's paper backing and cut it out. Take the paper off and place the leaf, adhesive side down, on the wrong side of the scarf and press it. Cut the piece out. Make as many as you like.

7

To attach leaves on the stems, place the bottom of a leaf (or pair of leaves) on the stem and wrap the floral tape around the bottom a few times. Wrap on down the stem a ways to make a smooth join. Repeat for more leaves as desired.

For the Peach Rose

1

Cut a strip 4 x 20 inches (10.2 x 50.8 cm) from a rose-colored scarf, and the same size strip from the tulle.

2

Fold both strips in half lengthwise, wrong sides facing. Lay the folded scarf strip on a flat surface and place the folded tulle on top, but with the folded edge on the opposite side. The top of the rose will have the folded scarf edge and the raw tulle edge.

3

Along the bottom (the raw edge of the scarf and the folded edge of the tulle), machine baste the three strips together, leaving long thread tails. Fold under the short ends and stitch them to make narrow, single-fold hems. Then use the long thread tails to gather the long edge fairly tightly.

4

Complete the piece as for the Multicolor Rose, starting at step 4, or finish it as a brooch (see Scarf Corsage).

For the Carnation Flower

1

Cut out two 5-inch (12.7 cm) circles from two or three different scarves. Stack the circles in layers, alternating the colors.

2

Fold the circles in half and then roll the semicircles to make a point at the bottom. Punch a hole at the bottom through the point.

3

Run one end of 16-gauge wire through the hole and bend the end down 1 inch (2.5 cm). Wrap the bottom of the flower with the floral tape, as in step 5 of the Multicolor Rose instructions.

4

To fringe the petals, cut through the layers of the flower from the top down, being careful not to cut them in half; make the cuts no longer than ½ inch (1.3 cm).

5

Make and attach leaves, and finish the stem, as in steps 6 and 7 of the Multicolor Rose instructions.

For the Button-Center Flower

1

Enlarge the templates on page 122 and cut them out.

2

Following the manufacturer's instructions, iron fusible web on the wrong side of three different scarves, enough to cut out both templates from each scarf. Trace the templates onto the paper backing, and cut them out.

3

To make double-sided flower petals, remove the paper backing from each of the pieces cut in the previous step and place them on the wrong side of the same scarf. Press them and cut them out. You should have three large flower shapes and three small flower shapes.

4

Stack the pieces with the large flower shapes on the bottom and the smaller ones on top, placing the petals off center from each other (figure 1).

figure 1

5

Fold the flower stack in half and use the punch to make a hole in the center ½ inch (1.3 cm) above the fold. Fold in half in the other direction and punch another hole. The result will be four evenly spaced holes in the center of the flower.

6

Refold the flower stack in half and run a piece of 16-gauge wire through one set of matching holes, bending the wire over 1 inch (2.5 cm) (figure 2).

figure 2

7

Fold the stack in the other direction and run a piece of the 24-gauge wire through one hole and up through the fabrics into the center. Run the wire through one or several buttons (as you like and depending on the button size) then take the wire back down and through the last hole. Wrap the wire around itself under the flower.

8

Wrap the stem and place the leaves, following steps 5–7 of the Multicolor Rose instructions.

Scarf Corsage

The rose flower converts easily into a brooch:

 Make the flower petals as usual, but instead of stitching the gathered fabric to the wire, coil the fabric layers around it and hand sew them along the bottom to secure. Make the bottom as flat as you can.

- Cut a small circle from the scrap, large enough to cover the bottom circle of stitching and large enough to use as a base for the pin. About 2 inches (5.1 cm) should do it. Hand sew the felt in place around the center circle.

- Attach the pin back. Cut a small rectangle of felt to conceal the pin back and hand sew it in place (figure 3).

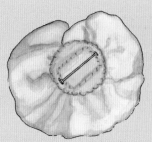

figure 3

Flicker

burn bright with these cute candleholders.

designed by Joan Morris

What You Do

1

Iron and starch the scarves, following the manufacturer's instructions. For each candleholder, do the following steps.

2

Measure the height and circumference of the candleholder. Add 1 inch (2.5 cm) to the top and bottom measurement (for two seam allowances) and add about 4 inches (10.2 cm) to the circumference, for ease of handling. Cut a piece that size from the scarf. If the scarf has a finished edge you like, make that the top edge and subtract one seam allowance from that side. Make a ½-inch (1.3 cm) single-fold hem (page 24) on the top and bottom edges, or make just one hem, if using a finished edge.

3

If using flat ribbon or trim for the embellishment, stitch it in place on the right side of the scarf piece, along the hemmed edges (beads, charms, or beaded ribbon will be stitched on later).

figure 1

What You Need

Assorted scarves, see Slim Pickings

Spray starch

Assorted embellishments, such as beaded ribbon, velvet ribbon, beads, or charms

Assorted glass candleholders

Basic Sewing Kit (page 14)

Needle nose pliers

Finished Size
Varies; the ones shown are 4–7 inches (10.2–17.8 cm) tall

Seam Allowance
½ inch (1.3 cm) unless otherwise noted

4

Wrap the hemmed scarf, wrong side out, around the candleholder. Pin it very tightly in place (figure 1). Slide the pinned piece off the candleholder and stitch a seam along the pin line, removing the pins as you go.

5

Finish the seam allowance by stitching a narrow, tight zigzag or satin stitch close to the seam. Trim off the seam allowance as close as possible to the satin stitch.

6

Turn the piece right side out and slide it onto the candleholder. It will be a tight fit, which is exactly what you want.

7

To add beads or charms, hand sew them in place along the top hem.

8

To add beaded ribbon, leave the scarf in place and wrap the ribbon around the candleholder. Mark where the seam needs to be and unwrap to hand sew the ends together. Slide the loop onto the holder and hand sew it in place. Use needle nose pliers, if needed, to pull the needle through the scarf and the beaded ribbon.

Slim Pickings

Narrow scarves—the ones 4 to 6 inches (10.2 to 15.2 cm) wide—are perfect for this project.

Charmed

a wind chime tinkles
in the slightest
summer breeze...

◇◇◇◇◇◇◇◇◇◇◇◇◇◇◇◇◇

designed by Valerie Van Arsdale Shrader

What You Do

1

For the framed pieces, cut the scarves into pieces a little larger than the frames. Apply decoupage medium to the backs of the frames and place the scarf pieces on top, right side down. Smooth them into the decoupage medium and apply another coat on top of the scarf pieces, pressing each firmly against the frame.

2

Let each piece dry, and then trim away the extra fabric.

3

For the banners, cut strips from the scarves that are about as wide as the frames. [The longest banner in this piece measures 7 inches (17.8 cm).] Wrap one end through the frame and stitch to secure it; use a backstitch for strength. Add a frame at the opposite end in the same way, to add a little weight to the banner.

4

Tie the banners onto the stick with long pieces of metallic floss, leaving the ends free and long if you wish. (It adds a little extra sparkle.)

5

Add the framed pieces to the stick in the same manner as the banners, arranging them as you like.

6

Use a short length of scarf to tie the chain onto the stick, threading the scarf through one of the links at either end of the chain. Or instead of a chain, you could use scarf remnants as the hanging mechanism.

What You Need

2 or 3 scarves in complementary colorways

18 large jewelry findings with metal frames

Decoupage medium

Cool-looking stick

Metallic embroidery floss

Decorative chain for the hanger, 20 inches (50.8 cm)

Basic Sewing Kit (page 14)

Small paintbrush

Templates

Bloom, page 114
Enlarge 200%

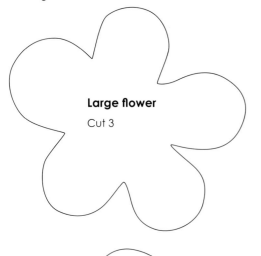

Large flower
Cut 3

Small flower
Cut 3

Use Your Head, page 85
Enlarge 300%

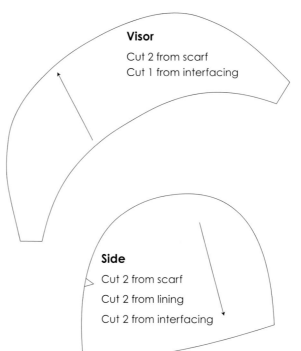

Visor
Cut 2 from scarf
Cut 1 from interfacing

Side
Cut 2 from scarf
Cut 2 from lining
Cut 2 from interfacing

Top
Cut 2 from scarf
Cut 2 from lining
Cut 2 from interfacing

Band
Cut 2 from second scarf

Hoppy, page 77

Enlarge 200%

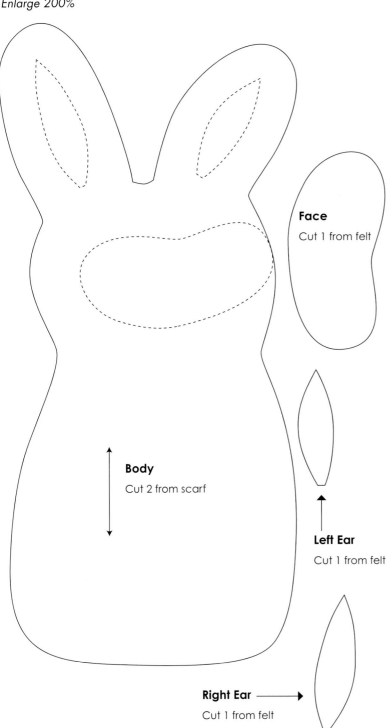

Face
Cut 1 from felt

Body
Cut 2 from scarf

Left Ear
Cut 1 from felt

Right Ear →
Cut 1 from felt

Kashmir, page 105

Enlarge 400%

Cut 4 pieces out of felt panel

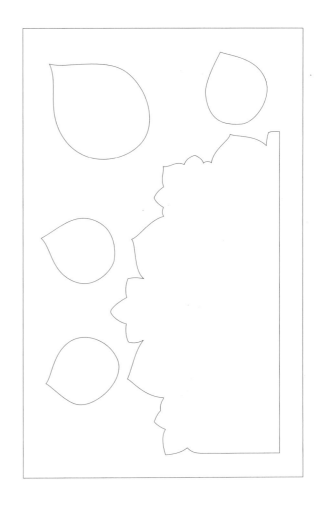

Bon Voyage, page 74

Enlarge 300%

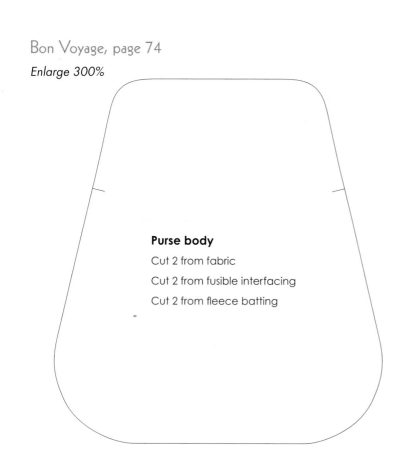

Purse body

Cut 2 from fabric

Cut 2 from fusible interfacing

Cut 2 from fleece batting

Waisting Time, page 65

Enlarge 200%

Cut 2 from stabilizer

Cut 2 from fusible web

Cut 2 from fabric (after fusing)

Cut on fold

Whisper, page 62

Actual size

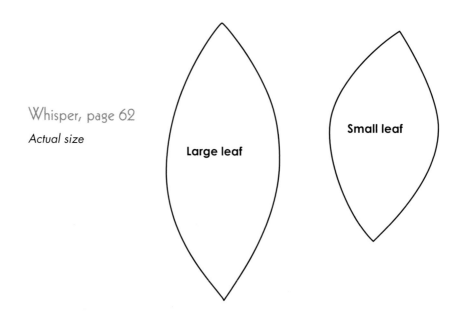

Large leaf

Small leaf

Shorty, page 30
Enlarge 400%

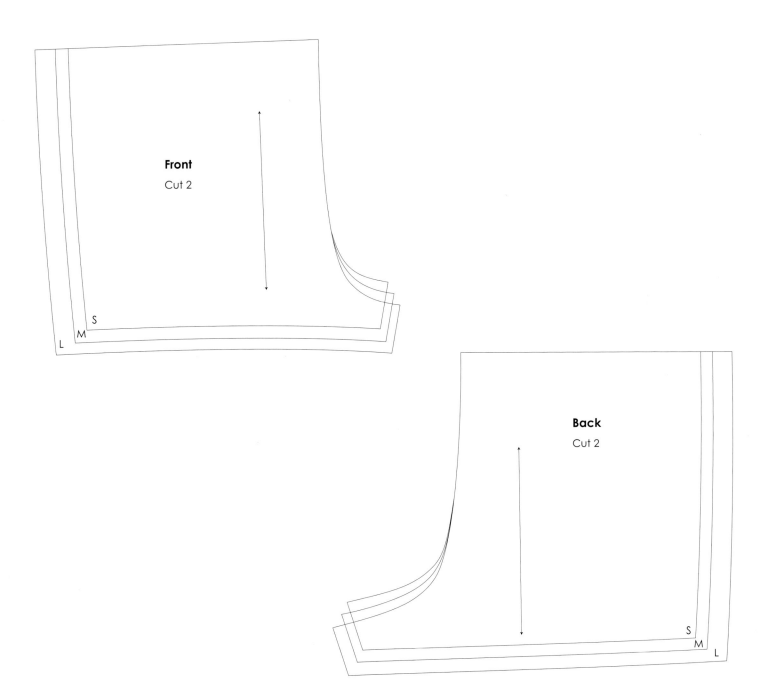

Front
Cut 2

S
M
L

Back
Cut 2

S
M
L

About the Designers

AMANDA CARESTIO'S latest crafting obsessions are mini quilts and furniture makeovers. When she's not bent over her sewing machine or exploring the Blue Ridge Mountains, Amanda enjoys spending quality time with her hubby and super-spoiled canines in Asheville, North Carolina. A member of Lark's Needlearts team, she is the author of *Fa La La La Felt*. Her designs appear in several other Lark books; see more of her creative distractions online at www.digsandbean.blogspot.com.

Stay-at-home mom **SAVANNAH CARROLL** runs the small, handmade business Sleepy King. When she's not sewing you'll find her gardening, cooking, or at the park. She's all about living green—from eating fresh and local organic food to buying handmade items. Savannah has a growing collection of porcelain miniature animals and is always on the lookout for handmade soaps. Stay current on her vintage finds, latest work, and family life at her blog www.misssleepyking.blogspot.com and visit her shop online at www.sleepyking.etsy.com.

CASEY DWYER, the owner of The Candy Thief, lives in the Adirondack Mountains in upstate New York, where she's able to work in her studio and enjoy the beautiful scenery every day. She sells her lovely wares online at www.thecandythief.etsy.com.

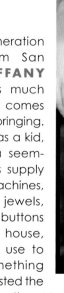

KERRI LAIDLAW is a self-confessed hoarder of fabrics, collecting anything textile with a vintage, kitsch, or retro edge. Having a two-bedroom apartment means getting creative when finding space to design and create bags and brooches. Kerri loves the creativity of sewing, designing, and trawling shops and garage sales for genuine vintage fabrics. She finds independence in selling her handmade products both face-to-face at markets and online. She's a member of the craft community group BrisStyle, an Etsy street team for designers and makers of products in Brisbane, Australia. Check out her adventures on her personal blog www.lampandmotor.blogspot.com and see some of her creations at her website www.lampandmotor.etsy.com.

A fourth-generation crafter from San Diego, **TIFFANY LAING** says much of her talent comes from her upbringing. When she was a kid, there was a seemingly endless supply of sewing machines, glue guns, jewels, beads, and buttons around the house, available to use to create something cool. She enlisted the help of her mother, Marie Fresh, to make the belt for this book. Tiffany finds things for her own daughter Vivian to "help" with; after all, Vivian may become the next generation of designer in this crafty family. Shop for Tiffany Laing merchandise at www.contrivedtocharm.etsy.com and www.glassbuttonbabe.etsy.com.

CATHY LANDRY specializes in sustainable women's clothing and accessories, selling her designs at several chic boutiques throughout the United States and Canada. Many of the designs for her label, Tangente, repurpose scarves into unique, one-of-a-kind tank tops and halters. When sewing is momentarily set aside, Cathy whips up new recipes, tends to her organic garden, and crafts funky home accessories. Cathy lives

in Ottawa, Canada, with her husband and three slightly overweight cats, and lets people into her craft world at her blog www.tangentedesigns.blogspot.com. You can also see her creations at www.tangente.etsy.com.

RACHEL LE GRAND, a married, stay-at-home mother of three from Minnesota, likes to divide her free time into various creative avenues. You might find her crafting in her turquoise studio, figuring out new ideas on how to repurpose jars, or on a scavenger hunt in vintage shops looking for hidden treasures. Rachel lived in France for more than three years where she learned how to wear scarves the chic way. See her latest ideas and designs at her craft blog www.nestfullofeggs.blogspot.com.

LILY+AMY is a mother/daughter team that creates hip T-shirts for the whole family. They believe in the handmade touch, which is why they hand-cut vintage fabric, hand alter, or crochet their own panels for each shirt they make. Living together in Brooklyn, New York, they share a two-family home full of children, grandchildren, spouses, and cats. Take a look at their shirt designs at www.starsandinfinitedarkness.com.

DAWN LIVERA started her creative clothing design as a young girl, making clothes for her dolls. As a teen, Dawn began re-making old clothing into original outfits. She was amused that the fashion world caught up to her style when it discovered altered couture. After having lived and traveled on three continents, she has finally settled down; she calls Vancouver, Canada, home. To learn more about Dawn, her interests, and other works she has created, visit www.aspotofserendip.wordpress.com.

An editor from Derbyshire, in the United Kingdom, **SUSAN MANTHORPE** runs a small online business in her spare time. No one would believe she's a self-taught seamstress after seeing her collection of handbags and cushions. Susan has a passion for vintage clothes, textiles, and jewelry. To see her unique pieces, visit her store at www.missmarmalade.co.uk.

JOAN MORRIS'S artistic endeavors have led her down many successful, creative paths, including ceramics and costume design for motion pictures. Joan has contributed projects to numerous Lark books, including *Quilt It with Wool* (2010), *Absolutely A-Line* (2009), *Pushing the Envelope* (2009), and *Craft Challenge: Dozens of Ways to Repurpose a Pillowcase* (2009).

ALICE PINO-MARINA'S creative style can be attributed to her mother, who made tons of clothes for her daughters when they were children. With a full house—a young son, a husband, and four dogs—Alice somehow finds time to create distinctive and eclectic pieces including coats, suitcases, necklaces, and knit wraps, to name a few. To see Alice's work, visit her website at www.vintagemarmalade.etsy.com.

JAMIE POWELL lives and works in Durham, North Carolina, where she produces her eco-conscious clothing line, Revamp. Her first-ever sewing project was for a Girl Scouts project, and once her mother taught her how to sew on their olive-green 1970s Sears sewing machine, she never stopped. After graduating from Appalachian State University with a degree in Business Administration, Jamie co-founded a vintage-clothing wholesaling business. Learning the trade helped foster the growth of her clothing line. Visit Jamie's online store at www. revampclothing.com.

Born and raised in Brooklyn, New York, **MARILYN SAQQAL** was taught how to sew by the women in her family—her grandmothers and her mother. Now living in Mahopac, New York, a village an hour's drive north of New York City, Marilyn takes the time to enjoy the Adirondacks and Lake George whenever she gets the chance. A mother of two and grandmother of four, she's the office manager in the law office of her husband, an attorney and sports agent. Marilyn finds time to make her creative pieces when she's not at work or fussing over the kids. When not designing and hand crafting felted handbags, fabric headbands, bracelets, and other creations, Marilyn likes to oil paint on canvas. She has also found an innovative way to use paper comic strips to make beads for necklaces. To see Marilyn's work, visit her website at www. handcraftusa.etsy.com.

LISA SCHIFFLEGER is quite the quilt lover. She spent childhood vacations visiting her grandparents in Mississippi, where her grandmother Lena made beautiful quilts, and seeing her love for them gave Lisa an appreciation for fabrics and quilting. She later learned from a friend the power of thrift shopping, and now gets more enjoyment sorting through textiles in second-hand stores than buying things new. Lisa currently lives in West Plains, Missouri. With her three children grown, she has more time to spend sewing and making quilts, and working toward fulfilling her simple dream of sewing for a living.

VALERIE VAN ARSDALE SHRADER made a pair of pink culottes when she was eleven and has loved fabric ever since. She's on the staff of Lark Crafts and has written and edited many books related to textiles and needlework. Valerie knits every now and then, too, and dreams about dyeing her own fabric and making art quilts.

RIVER TAKADA-CAPEL, a 2009 graduate of Haywood Community College's Professional Craft Program in Fiber, owns a business called Riverbasin Outfitters. The store

is an accumulation of clothing and accessory designs where everything is Eco.Eco.—River's term, meaning ecologically and economically friendly. She believes in teaching people about clothing, from making to altering, so that others can develop their own creative style and gain more confidence in the process. Now living back home in Chapel Hill, North Carolina, she's letting her creativity reach new heights. Check out a photo look book of her creations at www.riverbasinoutfitters.com.

RUTH TOWER, a pretty average thirty-something from Phoenix, Arizona, was inspired by her friend Andrea to take lonely vintage scarves and modernize them into useful hair accessories. She goes on the hunt at thrift shops regularly, searching for all things old and wonderful. Ruth keeps things simple by working mostly in the sewing and cross-stitch realms. Take a look at Ruth and Andrea's period finds at www.stores.ebay.com/annieboomervintage.

BETH WALKER is a powerhouse when it comes to making all things creative. She sews, embroiders, and knits original and quirky accessories. She also draws and writes and has published several works, including an essay, short stories, and a book. Beth lives in Boulder, Colorado, and labels her creations Ask a Marmot Designs. Contact her at beth@askamarmot.com.

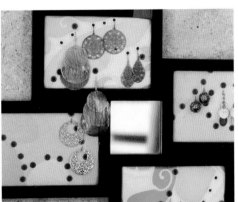

JUDIT WILD studied photojournalism and sociology in Hungary before jumping into the world of jewelry making in 2002. Today she divides her time between work as a media sociologist and as a jewelry designer. Her love for creating unique pieces drives her to find a way to combine different materials like glass, metal, and fabric into pieces of jewelry. People have started calling her Vadjutka, after her jewelry line. To learn more about Judit and her work, visit her website at www.vadjutka.hu/eng.

CYNTHIA B. WULLER has a BFA from the School of the Art Institute of Chicago. Besides being a jewelry designer and published author, she sells pet slings she makes from recycled fabric. She lives in Chicago with her husband and tiny Chihuahua, Matilda. The inspiration for her label, called Matilda Ware, comes—no surprise—from her dog.

About the Author

Nathalie Mornu works as an editor at Lark Crafts. She's dabbled in many crafts over the years, so as a sideline she sometimes creates projects for Lark publications—stuff as varied as stitched pot holders, beaded jewelry, a re-upholstered mid-century chair, a weird scarecrow made from cutlery, and a gingerbread igloo. Her author credits include *Quilt It with Wool* (2009), the best-selling *A Is for Apron* (2008), and *Cutting-Edge Decoupage* (2007). For her most recent book, *Leather Jewelry* (2010), she learned on the fly and made a handful of projects. Since discovering leather as a craft material, Nathalie has been filled with regret for all the years she could have spent building a hoard of breath-taking skins and creating magic with them.

Acknowledgments

Many people deserve praise for their work on this book, but none more than the designers who made the projects contained in its pages. Thank you all for your enthusiasm and for your willingness to share your bountiful imaginations!

Gratitude to Dana Irwin, who suggested scarves as a topic for this third *Craft Challenge* book. Thanks, too, to Kathleen McCafferty, a woman of many hats, who donned her deerstalker to sleuth these talented designers.

Technical editor extraordinaire Nancy Wood polished up the instructions provided by the designers, and did a whole lot more besides. Bernadette Wolf created the exquisite watercolor illustrations (aren't they the sweetest thing?). Orrin Lundgren, our go-to man for templates, did his thing. Editorial intern Allie Mathews came along for the ride, working like a pro on various aspects of the book.

Kudos to the Megans in the art department—Megan Kirby and Meagan Shirlen—who hunted high and low for adorable models, scouted far and wide for ideal locations, and shopped 'til they dropped for the perfect props and accessories to set off the projects.

Two thumbs up to photographer Lynne Harty; she makes every shot gorgeous! Hair and make-up maestro E. Scott Thompson made the models sparkle (as if they needed help). Ah, yes, the delightful models: Meredith (may she make it in show biz), Gretchen (may she win many pageants), Laura (can you believe this was her first shoot ever?!), and the terrific twosome, Morghyan and Lorya.

And how about that canine cuteness on page 82? Thanks to little Kobe, who appears in those photos courtesy of his owner, Duncan Rice.

Index

Bonus Projects

If you haven't had your fill of repurposed scarf projects, check out www.larkcrafts.com/bonus for two more freebies.

BONUS PROJECT
Toss Up
available **free** at
larkcrafts.com/bonus

BONUS PROJECT
Picture Perfect
available **free** at
larkcrafts.com/bonus

Also In This Series

Liberate pillowcases from humble bedding!

Is it a pillowcase or

...a darling sundress?

...a retro-chic, eco-friendly lunchbox?

...a cool superhero cape?

That's up to you, super-crafty sewer! Take the craft challenge and turn an ordinary pillowcase into an amazing and inventive something else. In *Craft Challenge: Dozens of Ways to Repurpose a Pillowcase*, you'll find 28 projects that will be profoundly transformative for you—and those bed linens!

WHEN IS A PILLOWCASE ANYTHING BUT A PILLOWCASE?

SHOW! Make it a totally cute candy-colored purse.

WEAR! Give it fun flair as a flirty ruffled apron.

LIVE! Crochet strips of pillow into a pretty striped bowl.

Tea towels aren't just for afternoon garden parties!

Is it a tea towel or

...the sweetest apron ever?

...a mod grocery bag?

...a pair of vacation-themed slippers?

It's in your hands, über-visionary sewer! These pretty linens are loaded with potential as craft canvases thanks to their fabulous colors and vintage appeal. The 28 projects contained in *Craft Challenge: Dozens of Ways to Repurpose a Tea Towel*, liberate tea towels from attics, yard sales, and thrift stores, and refashion them into equally adorable yet totally different little items.

WHEN IS A TEA TOWEL ANYTHING BUT A TEA TOWEL?

WEAR! Fashion it into an irresistibly girly mini skirt.

FLAUNT! Give it a touch of kitsch as an owl-shaped clock.

PLAY! Turn it into a cuddly doll.